MEDITERRANEAN
DIET COOKBOOK
FOR BEGINNERS

**150+ Quick & Easy Recipes for No-Stress Cooking
Full-Color Dishes, 30-Day Meal Plan, and Healthy Lifestyle
Weeknight Dinners**

MONIKA LAW

TABLE OF CONTENTS:

INTRODUCTION TO THE MEDITERRANEAN DIET

WELCOME, DEAR READER, TO A WORLD WHERE THE AZURE WATERS OF THE MEDITERRANEAN SEA KISS SUN-DRENCHED SHORES, AND THE AIR IS FRAGRANT WITH THE AROMA OF OLIVE GROVES AND CITRUS ORCHARDS. YOU ARE ABOUT TO EMBARK ON A CULINARY ODYSSEY THAT PROMISES A FEAST FOR YOUR TASTE BUDS AND A JOURNEY TOWARD A HEALTHIER, MORE VIBRANT YOU.

THIS COOKBOOK IS YOUR COMPASS TO NAVIGATING THE WHOLESOME AND DELECTABLE CUISINE OF THE MEDITERRANEAN DIET, RENOWNED FOR ITS HEART-HEALTHY BENEFITS AND ITS ROLE IN PROMOTING LONGEVITY. AS A BEGINNER, YOU MAY WONDER HOW TO INCORPORATE THIS DIET'S RICH FLAVORS AND DIVERSE INGREDIENTS INTO YOUR DAILY LIFE. FEAR NOT, FOR WE HAVE DESIGNED THIS GUIDE TO BE YOUR FRIENDLY COMPANION, LEADING YOU THROUGH THE BASICS WITH EASE AND JOY.

EACH CHAPTER UNFOLDS LIKE A NEW PORT OF CALL, INVITING YOU TO EXPLORE SIMPLE YET FLAVORFUL RECIPES THAT CELEBRATE THE FRESH PRODUCE, LEAN PROTEINS, AND HEALTHY FATS THAT ARE THE CORNERSTONES OF MEDITERRANEAN EATING. FROM THE SUN-KISSED HILLS OF TUSCANY TO THE BUSTLING MARKETS OF MARRAKECH, YOU'LL DISCOVER DISHES THAT WILL TRANSPORT YOU TO THESE EXOTIC LOCALES WITHOUT LEAVING YOUR KITCHEN. SO, TIE ON YOUR APRON, AND LET'S SET SAIL. YOUR ADVENTURE INTO THE HEART OF THE MEDITERRANEAN KITCHEN BEGINS NOW. WHO KNOWS WHAT DELICIOUS DISCOVERIES LIE AHEAD?

TOP 10 BENEFITS OF A MEDITERRANEAN DIET

1. HEALTHIER HEART: THE MEDITERRANEAN DIET IS RENOWNED FOR PROMOTING HEART HEALTH BY EMPHASIZING FRUITS, VEGETABLES, WHOLE GRAINS, AND HEALTHY FATS LIKE OLIVE OIL, WHICH CAN HELP LOWER CHOLESTEROL LEVELS AND REDUCE THE RISK OF HEART DISEASE.

2. WEIGHT MANAGEMENT: THIS DIET ENCOURAGES A BALANCED APPROACH TO EATING, FOCUSING ON NUTRIENT-DENSE FOODS AND PORTION CONTROL, WHICH CAN AID IN WEIGHT MANAGEMENT AND EVEN WEIGHT LOSS WHEN COMBINED WITH REGULAR PHYSICAL ACTIVITY.

3. REDUCED RISK OF CHRONIC DISEASES: STUDIES HAVE SHOWN THAT FOLLOWING A MEDITERRANEAN-STYLE DIET CAN LOWER THE RISK OF DEVELOPING CHRONIC DISEASES SUCH AS TYPE 2 DIABETES, CERTAIN CANCERS, AND NEURODEGENERATIVE DISORDERS LIKE ALZHEIMER'S DISEASE.

4. IMPROVED DIGESTIVE HEALTH: THE EMPHASIS ON FIBER-RICH FOODS SUCH AS FRUITS, VEGETABLES, AND WHOLE GRAINS IN THE MEDITERRANEAN DIET CAN PROMOTE HEALTHY DIGESTION, PREVENT CONSTIPATION, AND SUPPORT OVERALL GUT HEALTH.

5. INCREASED ANTIOXIDANT INTAKE: THIS DIET'S ABUNDANCE OF FRUITS, VEGETABLES, NUTS, AND SEEDS PROVIDES A WIDE RANGE OF ANTIOXIDANTS THAT HELP PROTECT CELLS FROM OXIDATIVE STRESS AND REDUCE INFLAMMATION.

6. BETTER BRAIN FUNCTION: THE MEDITERRANEAN DIET HAS BEEN ASSOCIATED WITH IMPROVED COGNITIVE FUNCTION, MEMORY, AND MOOD, THANKS TO THE CONSUMPTION OF OMEGA-3 FATTY ACIDS FROM FISH, AS WELL AS ANTIOXIDANTS FROM FRUITS AND VEGETABLES.

7. LONGEVITY: STUDIES SUGGEST THAT ADHERING TO A MEDITERRANEAN-STYLE EATING PATTERN IS LINKED TO INCREASED LONGEVITY AND A LOWER RISK OF PREMATURE DEATH, POSSIBLY DUE TO ITS HEALTH-PROMOTING EFFECTS.

8. BALANCED NUTRIENT INTAKE: THE DIET ENCOURAGES A BALANCE OF MACRONUTRIENTS, INCLUDING HEALTHY FATS FROM OLIVE OIL AND OMEGA-3 FATTY ACIDS FROM FISH, CARBOHYDRATES FROM WHOLE GRAINS, AND PROTEIN FROM LEAN SOURCES SUCH AS POULTRY AND LEGUMES.

9. DELICIOUS AND VARIED MEALS: A MEDITERRANEAN DIET COOKBOOK FOR BEGINNERS INTRODUCES A WIDE RANGE OF FLAVORFUL RECIPES USING FRESH INGREDIENTS, HERBS, AND SPICES THAT CAN MAKE HEALTHY EATING ENJOYABLE AND SUSTAINABLE.

10. EASY TO FOLLOW: THE MEDITERRANEAN DIET IS NOT ABOUT STRICT RULES OR DEPRIVATION BUT FOCUSES ON A FLEXIBLE AND ENJOYABLE APPROACH TO EATING, MAKING IT EASIER FOR BEGINNERS TO ADOPT AND MAINTAIN LONG-TERM DIETARY HABITS.

OVERALL, A MEDITERRANEAN DIET COOKBOOK FOR BEGINNERS OFFERS NUMEROUS BENEFITS FOR HEALTH, WELL-BEING, AND CULINARY ENJOYMENT, MAKING IT A POPULAR CHOICE FOR THOSE LOOKING TO IMPROVE THEIR EATING HABITS AND LIFESTYLE.

ESSENTIAL INGREDIENTS:

1. EXTRA VIRGIN OLIVE OIL: THIS IS A STAPLE OF MEDITERRANEAN CUISINE, USED FOR COOKING, SALAD DRESSINGS, AND FLAVORING VARIOUS DISHES.

2. WHOLE GRAINS: INCLUDE INGREDIENTS LIKE WHOLE WHEAT PASTA, BROWN RICE, QUINOA, BULGUR, AND BARLEY FOR FIBER, NUTRIENTS, AND SUSTAINED ENERGY.

3. FRESH VEGETABLES: STOCK UP ON FRESH VEGETABLES SUCH AS TOMATOES, CUCUMBERS, BELL PEPPERS, ONIONS, GARLIC, LEAFY GREENS, AND EGGPLANTS FOR SALADS, STEWS, AND SIDE DISHES.

4. LEAN PROTEINS: FOR A BALANCED DIET, INCORPORATE LEAN PROTEINS LIKE FISH (SALMON, SARDINES, TROUT), POULTRY (CHICKEN, TURKEY), LEGUMES (BEANS, LENTILS), AND OCCASIONALLY LEAN CUTS OF RED MEAT.

5. FRUITS: HAVE A SELECTION OF FRESH FRUITS, SUCH AS ORANGES, LEMONS, BERRIES, APPLES, AND FIGS, FOR SNACKS, DESSERTS, AND ADDING SWEETNESS TO SAVORY DISHES.

6. NUTS AND SEEDS: ADD ALMONDS, WALNUTS, PINE NUTS, SESAME SEEDS, AND FLAXSEEDS TO SALADS, SAUCES, AND BAKED GOODS FOR ADDED TEXTURE, FLAVOR, AND HEALTHY FATS.

7. HERBS AND SPICES: STOCK YOUR PANTRY WITH MEDITERRANEAN HERBS SUCH AS BASIL, OREGANO, THYME, ROSEMARY, AND PARSLEY AND SPICES LIKE CUMIN, PAPRIKA, CINNAMON, AND TURMERIC TO ENHANCE FLAVORS WITHOUT EXCESSIVE SALT.

8. SEAFOOD: INCORPORATE A VARIETY OF SEAFOOD OPTIONS, SUCH AS SHRIMP, MUSSELS, CLAMS, AND SQUID, FOR PROTEIN, OMEGA-3 FATTY ACIDS, AND A TASTE OF MEDITERRANEAN COASTAL CUISINE.

9. GREEK YOGURT AND CHEESE: GREEK YOGURT IS A CREAMY BASE FOR DIPS AND SAUCES, AND CHEESES LIKE FETA, RICOTTA, AND PARMESAN ADD RICHNESS AND FLAVOR.

10. LEGUMES AND PULSES: CHOOSE DRIED OR CANNED LEGUMES SUCH AS CHICKPEAS, KIDNEY BEANS, BLACK BEANS, AND LENTILS FOR PROTEIN-RICH SALADS, SOUPS, AND STEWS.

ESSENTIAL KITCHEN TOOLS:

1. QUALITY CHEF'S KNIFE: A SHARP, HIGH-QUALITY CHEF'S KNIFE IS ESSENTIAL FOR CHOPPING VEGETABLES, FRUITS, HERBS, AND PROTEINS EFFICIENTLY.

2. CUTTING BOARD: USE A STURDY WOOD OR PLASTIC CUTTING BOARD TO PROTECT YOUR COUNTERTOPS AND PROVIDE A STABLE SURFACE FOR FOOD PREP.

3. NON-STICK SKILLET OR PAN: A NON-STICK SKILLET OR PAN IS HANDY FOR COOKING WITH MINIMAL OIL AND PREPARING DISHES LIKE SAUTÉED VEGETABLES, FISH FILLETS, AND OMELETS.

4. BAKING SHEET: A LARGE BAKING SHEET IS HELPFUL FOR ROASTING VEGETABLES, BAKING FISH, AND MAKING HOMEMADE WHOLE-GRAIN BREAD OR FLATBREADS.

5. SALAD SPINNER: A SALAD SPINNER HELPS RINSE AND DRY LEAFY GREENS AND HERBS QUICKLY, ENSURING CRISP AND FRESH SALADS.

6. BLENDER OR FOOD PROCESSOR: BLENDERS AND FOOD PROCESSORS MAKE SMOOTHIES, SAUCES, DIPS, AND PURÉES QUICKLY.

7. CITRUS JUICER: A CITRUS JUICER OR REAMER EXTRACTS FRESH LEMON, LIME, AND ORANGE JUICE FOR SALAD DRESSINGS, MARINADES, AND BEVERAGES.

8. GRATER/ZESTER: HAVE A GRATER OR ZESTER ON HAND FOR GRATING CHEESE, ZESTING CITRUS FRUITS, AND ADDING FLAVOR TO DISHES WITH GRATED GARLIC OR GINGER.

9. MEASURING CUPS AND SPOONS: ACCURATE MEASURING CUPS AND SPOONS ARE ESSENTIAL FOR FOLLOWING RECIPES AND PORTION CONTROL WHEN COOKING AND BAKING.

10. MIXING BOWLS: HAVE A SET OF MIXING BOWLS IN VARIOUS SIZES FOR COMBINING INGREDIENTS, MARINATING PROTEINS, AND TOSSING SALADS

• SALTY BREAKFAST •

GREEK SCRAMBLED EGGS (STRAPATSADA)

INGREDIENTS

- 4 large eggs
- 1 tomato, diced
- 1/4 cup feta cheese, crumbled
- 1/4 cup fresh parsley, chopped
- Salt and pepper to taste
- 2 tablespoons olive oil

2

10 mins

10 mins

DIRECTIONS

1. In a bowl, whisk the eggs until well beaten—season with salt and pepper.

2. Heat olive oil in a non-stick skillet over medium heat. Add diced tomatoes and cook until softened.

3. Pour the beaten eggs into the skillet with the tomatoes. Stir gently until the eggs start to set.

4. Add crumbled feta cheese and chopped parsley to the skillet. Continue stirring until the eggs are cooked to your desired consistency.

5. Remove from heat and serve hot.

Nutritional Information (per serving): 348 calories, 21g protein, 7g carbohydrates, 26g fat, 2g fiber, 426mg cholesterol, 393mg sodium, 316mg potassium.

MEDITERRANEAN VEGGIE OMELETTE

INGREDIENTS

2
10 mins
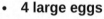

- 4 large eggs
- 1/2 cup cherry tomatoes, halved
- 1/2 cup baby spinach, chopped
- 1/4 cup red bell pepper, diced
- 1/4 cup feta cheese, crumbled
- Salt and pepper to taste
- 2 tablespoons olive oil

DIRECTIONS

1. In a bowl, whisk the eggs until well beaten. Season with salt and pepper.

2. Heat olive oil in a non-stick skillet over medium heat. Add cherry tomatoes, baby spinach, and red bell pepper. Cook until vegetables are tender.

3. Pour the beaten eggs over the cooked vegetables in the skillet. Swirl the pan to distribute the eggs evenly.

4. Sprinkle crumbled feta cheese on top of the omelet. Cook until the edges start to set and the bottom is golden brown.

5. Carefully fold the omelet in half using a spatula. Cook for another minute to ensure the eggs are fully cooked.

Nutritional Information (per serving): 352 calories, 19g protein, 7g carbohydrates, 28g fat, 2g fiber, 426mg cholesterol, 398mg sodium, 328mg potassium.

QUINOA BREAKFAST BOWL

INGREDIENTS

- 1/2 cup quinoa, rinsed
- 1 cup water or vegetable broth
- 1 avocado, sliced
- 1 cup cherry tomatoes, halved
- 4 large eggs
- 1 tablespoon olive oil
- Salt and pepper to taste
- Optional toppings: feta cheese, chopped fresh herbs, hot sauce

2

10 mins

15 mins

DIRECTIONS

1. Combine quinoa and water or vegetable broth in a saucepan. Bring to a boil, then reduce heat to low, cover, and simmer for about 15 minutes, or until quinoa is tender and liquid is absorbed.
2. While quinoa is cooking, heat olive oil in a nonstick skillet over medium heat. Crack the eggs into the skillet and cook until the whites are set but the yolks are still runny, or cook to your desired doneness.
3. Divide cooked quinoa between two bowls. Top with sliced avocado, cherry tomatoes, and the boiled eggs.
4. Season with salt and pepper to taste.
5. Add optional toppings like crumbled feta cheese, chopped fresh herbs, or hot sauce if desired.

Nutritional Information (per serving): 438 calories, 17g protein, 35g carbohydrates, 27g fat, 8g fiber, 186mg cholesterol, 182mg sodium, 729mg potassium.

SMOKED SALMON PLATE

INGREDIENTS

2

10 mins

0 mins

- 4 oz smoked salmon
- 4 hard-boiled eggs, sliced
- 1 avocado, sliced
- 1 cup mixed salad greens
- 1 tablespoon capers
- Lemon wedges for serving
- Salt and pepper to taste
- Optional: whole grain crackers or bread

DIRECTIONS

1. Arrange the mixed salad greens on a plate as the base.
2. Place slices of smoked salmon, hard-boiled eggs, and avocado on top of the greens.
3. Sprinkle capers over the salmon and avocado.
4. Season with salt and pepper to taste.
5. Serve with lemon wedges on the side and optional whole-grain crackers or bread.

Nutritional Information (per serving): 296 calories, 22g protein, 9g carbohydrates, 20g fat, 4g fiber, 384mg cholesterol, 932mg sodium, 730mg potassium.

AVOCADO TOAST

INGREDIENTS

- 2 slices whole grain bread
- 1 ripe avocado
- 1 small tomato, sliced
- 2 tablespoons red onion, finely chopped
- Salt and pepper to taste
- 1 tablespoon olive oil
- 1 tablespoon lemon juice
- Optional toppings: feta cheese, sliced radishes, sprouts

2

10 mins

15 mins

DIRECTIONS

1. Toast the whole grain bread slices until golden brown.
2. In a bowl, mash the ripe avocado with a fork. Add olive oil, lemon juice, salt, and pepper. Mix well.
3. Spread the mashed avocado evenly on the toasted bread slices.
4. Top the avocado toast with sliced tomatoes and chopped red onions.
5. Add optional toppings like feta cheese, sliced radishes, or sprouts if desired.

Nutritional Information (per serving): 305 calories, 7g protein, 27g carbohydrates, 20g fat, 9g fiber, 0mg cholesterol, 238mg sodium, 585mg potassium.

MEDITERRANEAN SHAKSHUKA

INGREDIENTS

2

10 mins

20 mins

- 4 large eggs
- 1 can (14.5 oz) diced tomatoes
- 1/2 onion, chopped
- 1 bell pepper, chopped
- 2 cloves garlic, minced
- 2 tablespoons olive oil
- 1 teaspoon ground cumin
- 1 teaspoon paprika, Salt and pepper to taste
- Fresh parsley or cilantro for garnish
- Optional: feta cheese, olives, crusty bread

DIRECTIONS

1. Heat olive oil in a skillet over medium heat. Add chopped onion, bell pepper, and minced garlic. Cook until softened, about 5 minutes.
2. Stir in ground cumin, paprika, salt, and pepper. Cook for another minute to toast the spices.
3. Pour in the diced tomatoes with their juices. Simmer for 10-15 minutes until the sauce thickens slightly.
4. Create wells in the tomato mixture using a spoon. Crack one egg into each well.

Cover the skillet and cook until the eggs are set to your liking, about 5-7 minutes. Garnish with fresh parsley or cilantro. Serve hot with optional toppings like crumbled feta cheese, olives, and crusty

Nutritional Information (per serving): 329 calories, 13g protein, 20g carbohydrates, 22g fat, 5g fiber, 372mg cholesterol, 537mg sodium, 607mg potassium.

HUMMUS BREAKFAST PLATE

INGREDIENTS

- 1 cup prepared hummus
- 2 hardboiled eggs, sliced
- 1/2 avocado, sliced
- 1/2 cup cherry tomatoes, halved
- 2 tablespoons chopped fresh parsley
- 1 tablespoon olive oil
- Salt and pepper to taste
- Optional toppings: feta cheese, olives, whole grain pita bread

2

10 mins

0 mins

DIRECTIONS

1. Spread the prepared hummus evenly on two plates.
2. Arrange sliced hardboiled eggs, avocado slices, and cherry tomatoes on top of the hummus.
3. Drizzle olive oil over the ingredients.
4. Season with salt and pepper to taste.
5. Sprinkle chopped fresh parsley on top.
6. Serve the hummus breakfast plate with optional toppings like crumbled feta cheese, olives, or whole grain pita bread.

Nutritional Information (per serving): 478 calories, 17g protein, 28g carbohydrates, 36g fat, 11g fiber, 372mg cholesterol, 555mg sodium, 867mg potassium.

MEDITERRANEAN BREAKFAST WRAP

INGREDIENTS

2

10 mins

5 mins

- 2 large wholegrain tortillas
- 4 large eggs
- 1/2 cup baby spinach leaves
- 1/2 cup diced tomatoes
- 1/4 cup crumbled feta cheese
- 1 tablespoon olive oil
- Salt and pepper to taste
- Optional toppings: sliced avocado, Greek Yogurt, hot sauce

DIRECTIONS

1. In a bowl, whisk the eggs until well beaten—season with salt and pepper.
2. Heat olive oil in a nonstick skillet over medium heat. Add the beaten eggs and scramble until cooked through.
3. Warm the whole grain tortillas in a separate skillet or microwave.
4. Evenly Divide the scrambled eggs, baby spinach, diced tomatoes, and crumbled feta cheese between the two tortillas.
5. Roll up the tortillas to form wraps.
6. Optional: Serve with sliced avocado, a dollop of Greek Yogurt, or a drizzle of hot sauce.

Nutritional Information (per serving): 391 calories, 20g protein, 29g carbohydrates, 22g fat, 6g fiber, 380mg cholesterol, 613mg sodium, 464mg potassium

FETA AND OLIVE FRITTATA

INGREDIENTS

- 4 large eggs
- 1/4 cup crumbled feta cheese
- 1/4 cup sliced black olives
- 1/4 cup diced red bell pepper
- 2 tablespoons chopped fresh parsley
- Salt and pepper to taste
- 1 tablespoon olive oil

2

10 mins

15mins

DIRECTIONS

1. In a bowl, whisk the eggs until well beaten. Stir in crumbled feta cheese, sliced black olives, diced red bell pepper, chopped fresh parsley, salt, and pepper.

2. Heat olive oil in a nonstick skillet over medium heat.

3. Pour the egg mixture into the skillet and spread evenly.

4. Cook the frittata for 10-12 minutes until the edges are set and the top is slightly firm.

5. Carefully flip the frittata using a spatula and cook for another 34 minutes until cooked.

Nutritional Information (per serving): 297 calories, 18g protein, 5g carbohydrates, 23g fat, 1g fiber, 419mg cholesterol, 628mg sodium, 226mg potassium.

GREEK YOGURT WITH HONEY AND NUTS

INGREDIENTS

- 2 cup Greek yogurt
- 2 tablespoons honey
- 1/2 cup mixed nuts (such as almonds, walnuts, or pistachios), chopped

2

5 mins

0 mins

DIRECTIONS

1. In two serving bowls, divide the Greek Yogurt evenly.
2. Drizzle one tablespoon of honey over each portion of Yogurt.
3. Sprinkle chopped mixed nuts on top of the honeyed Yogurt.
4. Serve immediately as a nutritious and delicious breakfast or snack.

Nutritional Information (per serving): 263 calories, 15g protein, 19g carbohydrates, 15g fat, 2g fiber, 15mg cholesterol, 36mg sodium, 238mg potassium.

OATMEAL WITH MEDITERRANEAN TOPPINGS

INGREDIENTS

2

5 mins

10 mins

- 1 cup rolled oats
- 2 cups water or milk of choice
- Pinch of salt
- 1/2 cup sliced almonds
- 1/4 cup dried apricots, chopped
- 1/4 cup raisins
- 2 tablespoons honey or maple syrup
- 1/2 teaspoon ground cinnamon
- Optional toppings: fresh berries, Greek Yogurt, chia seeds

DIRECTIONS

1. Combine rolled oats, water or milk, and a pinch of salt in a saucepan. Bring to a boil, then reduce heat to low and simmer for about 5-7 minutes, stirring occasionally, until oats are cooked and creamy.
2. While cooking oats, toast the sliced almonds in a dry skillet over medium heat until lightly golden and fragrant, about 3-4 minutes. Remove from heat and set aside.
3. Once the oats are cooked, stir in chopped dried apricots, raisins, honey or maple syrup, and ground cinnamon.
4. Divide the oatmeal between two serving bowls.
5. Top each bowl of oatmeal with toasted sliced almonds and any optional toppings like fresh berries, a dollop of Greek Yogurt, or a sprinkle of chia seeds.

Nutritional Information (per serving): 380 calories, 10g protein, 65g carbohydrates, 10g fat, 8g fiber, 0mg cholesterol, 2mg sodium, 380mg potassium.

ALMOND BUTTER AND BANANA TOAST

INGREDIENTS

- 4 slices whole grain bread
- 4 tablespoons almond butter
- 1 large banana, sliced
- Honey or maple syrup for drizzling (optional)
- Pinch of cinnamon (optional)

2

5 mins

5 mins

DIRECTIONS

1. Toast the whole grain bread slices until golden brown and crispy.
2. Spread two tablespoons of almond butter evenly on each slice of toasted bread.
3. Arrange banana slices on top of the almond butter.
4. Optional: Drizzle honey or maple syrup over the banana slices and sprinkle with a pinch of cinnamon for extra flavor.
5. Serve the almond butter and banana toast immediately as a delicious and nutritious breakfast or snack.

Nutritional Information (per serving): 324 calories, 9g protein, 43g carbohydrates, 14g fat, 7g fiber, 0mg cholesterol, 239mg sodium, 372mg potassium.

RICOTTA AND FIG TOAST

INGREDIENTS

2

5 mins

5 mins

- 4 slices whole grain bread
- 1/2 cup ricotta cheese
- 4 fresh figs, sliced
- Honey for drizzling (optional)
- Fresh thyme leaves for garnish (optional)

DIRECTIONS

1. Toast the whole grain bread slices until golden brown and crispy.
2. Spread 1/4 cup of ricotta cheese evenly on each slice of toasted bread.
3. Arrange sliced fresh figs on top of the ricotta cheese.
4. Optional: Drizzle honey over the figs for added sweetness.
5. Garnish with fresh thyme leaves for a touch of flavor and presentation.
6. Serve the ricotta and fig toast immediately as a delightful breakfast or snack.

Nutritional Information (per serving): 261 calories, 10g protein, 41g carbohydrates, 7g fat, 6g fiber, 25mg cholesterol, 255mg sodium, 372mg potassium.

HONEY SPICED GRANOLA WITH YOGURT

INGREDIENTS

- 1 cup oldfashioned oats
- 1/4 cup chopped almonds
- 1/4 cup chopped walnuts
- 2 tablespoons honey
- 1 tablespoon coconut oil, melted
- 1 teaspoon ground cinnamon
- 1/4 teaspoon ground nutmeg
- 1 cup Greek yogurt; Pinch of salt
- Fresh berries or sliced fruits for serving

2

10 mins

20 mins

DIRECTIONS

1. Preheat the oven to 325°F (163°C) and line a baking sheet with parchment paper.
2. In a large mixing bowl, combine the oldfashioned oats, chopped almonds, chopped walnuts, honey, melted coconut oil, ground cinnamon, ground nutmeg, and a pinch of salt. Mix until everything is wellcoated.
3. Spread the granola mixture evenly on the prepared baking sheet.
4. Bake in the preheated oven for about 15-20 minutes, stirring halfway through, until the granola is golden brown and crispy. Remove the granola from the oven and let it cool completely.
5. To serve, divide the Greek Yogurt between two bowls and top with the honeyspiced granola.
6. Add fresh berries or sliced fruits to the granola and Yogurt.
7. Enjoy the honeyspiced granola with Yogurt as a delicious and nutritious breakfast or snack.

Nutritional Information (per serving): 153 calories, 5g protein, 12g carbohydrates, 9g fat, 10g fiber, 0mg cholesterol, 87mg sodium, 150mg potassium.

BAKED APPLES WITH CINNAMON

INGREDIENTS

2

10 mins

25 mins

- 2 large apples (such as Honeycrisp or Granny Smith)
- 1 tablespoon melted butter or coconut oil
- 2 tablespoons honey or maple syrup
- 1 teaspoon ground cinnamon
- Optional toppings: chopped nuts, Greek Yogurt, granola

DIRECTIONS

1. Preheat the oven to 375°F (190°C).
2. Wash the apples and remove the cores using a corer or a sharp knife, leaving the bottoms intact.
3. Place the cored apples in a baking dish.
4. Mix melted butter or coconut oil, honey or maple syrup, and ground cinnamon in a small bowl.
5. Drizzle the cinnamon mixture over the apples and coat them evenly.
6. Bake the apples in the oven for about 25 minutes or until tender and lightly browned.
7. Remove the baked apples from the oven and let them cool slightly before serving.
8. Optional: Serve the baked apples with chopped nuts, a Greek Yogurt dollop, or a granola sprinkle on top.

Nutritional Information (per serving): 210 calories, 1g protein, 48g carbohydrates, 4g fat, 6g fiber, 10mg cholesterol, 2mg sodium, 265mg potassium.

MEDITERRANEAN STYLE PANCAKES

INGREDIENTS

- 1 cup allpurpose flour
- 1 tablespoon sugar
- 1 teaspoon baking powder
- 1/2 teaspoon ground cinnamon
- 1/4 teaspoon salt
- 1 cup milk
- 1 large egg
- 2 tablespoons olive oil
- 1 teaspoon vanilla extract
- Optional toppings: Greek Yogurt, honey, fresh berries, chopped nuts

2

10 mins

10 mins

DIRECTIONS

1. Combine the allpurpose flour, sugar, baking powder, ground cinnamon, and salt in a large mixing bowl.
2. Whisk together the milk, egg, olive oil, and vanilla extract in a separate bowl.
3. Pour the wet ingredients into the dry ingredients and stir until combined. Refrain from overmixing; it's okay if the batter is slightly lumpy.
4. Heat a nonstick skillet or griddle over medium heat and lightly grease with cooking spray or olive oil.
5. Pour about 1/4 cup of batter onto the skillet for each pancake. Cook until bubbles form on the surface of the pancake and the edges start to look set, about 2-3 minutes.
6. Flip the pancakes and cook for another 1-2 minutes until golden brown and cooked through.
7. Remove the pancakes from the skillet and repeat with the remaining batter.
8. Serve the Mediterraneanstyle pancakes warm with optional toppings like Greek Yogurt, honey, fresh berries, or chopped nuts.

Nutritional Information (per serving): 420 calories, 12g protein, 60g carbohydrates, 15g fat, 3g fiber,75mg cholesterol, 620mg sodium, 280mg potassium.

PISTACHIO AND HONEY TOAST

INGREDIENTS

2

5 mins

5 mins

- 4 slices whole grain bread
- 2 tablespoons pistachios, chopped
- 2 tablespoons honey
- Optional: 1 tablespoon unsalted butter

DIRECTIONS

1. If using, spread a thin layer of unsalted butter on each slice of wholegrain bread.
2. Toast the bread slices until golden brown and crispy.
3. Sprinkle chopped pistachios evenly over the toasted bread slices.
4. Drizzle one tablespoon of honey over each slice of toast.
5. Serve the pistachio and honey toast immediately as a delightful and nutritious breakfast or snack.

Nutritional Information (per serving): 280 calories, 6g protein, 50g carbohydrates, 8g fat, 5g fiber, 0mg cholesterol, 230mg sodium, 160mg potassium.

LEMON-RICOTTA PANCAKE BITES

INGREDIENTS

- 1 cup ricotta cheese; 1 large egg
- 1/2 cup milk (or almond milk); Zest of 1 lemon
- 1 tablespoon lemon juice; 1 teaspoon vanilla extract
- 1/2 cup all-purpose flour (or whole wheat flour for a healthier option)
- 1 tablespoon sugar
- 1/2 teaspoon baking powder; Pinch of salt
- Olive oil or butter for cooking
- Fresh berries and honey for serving

4

10 mins

15 mins

DIRECTIONS

1. In a medium bowl, whisk together the ricotta, egg, milk, lemon zest, lemon juice, and vanilla extract until smooth.
2. In a separate bowl, mix the flour, sugar, baking powder, and salt.
3. Gradually add the dry ingredients to the ricotta mixture, stirring until just combined (the batter will be thick).
4. Heat a skillet over medium heat and add a small amount of olive oil or butter.
5. Scoop about a tablespoon of batter onto the skillet for each pancake bite. Cook for 2–3 minutes per side, or until golden brown and cooked through.
6. Repeat with the remaining batter, adding more oil or butter as needed.
7. Serve warm, topped with fresh berries and a drizzle of honey.

Nutritional Information (per serving): 210 calories, 8g protein, 24g carbohydrates, 10g fat, 1g fiber, 48mg cholesterol, 160mg sodium, 95mg potassium.

SWEET COUSCOUS PORRIDGE WITH FRESH FIGS

INGREDIENTS

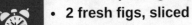

2

5 mins

10 mins

- 1/2 cup couscous
- 3/4 cup almond milk (or milk of choice)
- 1 tablespoon honey (or maple syrup)
- 1/2 teaspoon vanilla extract
- 1/4 teaspoon ground cinnamon
- 1/8 teaspoon ground cardamom (optional)
- 2 fresh figs, sliced
- 2 tablespoons chopped almonds or pistachios
- Additional honey for drizzling (optional)

DIRECTIONS

1. In a small saucepan, bring almond milk to a gentle simmer over medium heat.
2. Stir in the honey, vanilla extract, cinnamon, and cardamom (if using).
3. Add the couscous to the saucepan, stirring to combine. Cover and remove from heat. Let sit for 5 minutes, or until the couscous absorbs the milk and becomes tender.
4. Fluff the couscous with a fork, then divide it into two bowls.
5. Top with fresh fig slices, chopped nuts, and an optional drizzle of honey.

Nutritional Information (per serving): 220 calories, 6g protein, 32g carbohydrates, 9g fat, 3g fiber, 0mg cholesterol, 60mg sodium, 160mg potassium.

• SOUPS •

GREEK LEMON CHICKEN SOUP (AVGOLEMONO)

INGREDIENTS

- 2 cups lowsodium chicken broth
- 1 cup cooked chicken breast, shredded or diced
- 1/4 cup orzo pasta
- 2 large eggs
- 1/4 cup fresh lemon juice
- Salt and pepper to taste
- Fresh parsley for garnish

2

10 mins

20 mins

DIRECTIONS

1. Bring the chicken broth to a boil in a medium pot.
2. Add the orzo pasta to the boiling broth and cook according to package instructions until tender.
3. Whisk the eggs and lemon juice until well combined in a mixing bowl.
4. Once the orzo is cooked, reduce the heat to low and gradually pour a ladleful of hot broth from the pot into the egglemon mixture, whisking constantly to temper the eggs.
5. Slowly pour the egglemon mixture into the pot while stirring continuously to prevent curdling.
6. Add the cooked chicken to the soup and stir to combine—season with salt and pepper to taste.
7. Simmer the soup for a few more minutes until heated through.
8. Ladle the Greek Lemon Chicken Soup into serving bowls and garnish with fresh parsley before serving.

Nutritional Information (per serving): 282 calories, 24g protein, 19g carbohydrates, 11g fat, 1g fiber, 260mg cholesterol, 376mg sodium, 288mg potassium.

MEDITERRANEAN GAZPACHO SOUP

INGREDIENTS

2

15 mins

0 mins

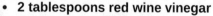

- 4 large tomatoes, chopped
- 1 cucumber, peeled and chopped
- 1 red bell pepper, chopped
- 1/2 red onion, chopped
- 2 cloves garlic, minced
- 2 tablespoons extra virgin olive oil
- 2 tablespoons red wine vinegar
- Salt and pepper to taste
- Optional: 1/4 teaspoon cayenne pepper for a spicy kick

DIRECTIONS

1. Combine the chopped tomatoes, cucumber, bell pepper, red onion, garlic, olive oil, and red wine vinegar in a blender. Blend until smooth.
2. Season with salt, pepper, and cayenne pepper if using. Blend again to incorporate the seasoning.
3. Transfer the gazpacho to a bowl, refrigerate for at least 1 hour, and allow the flavors to meld.
4. Serve the chilled gazpacho soup in bowls, garnished with a drizzle of olive oil and fresh herbs if desired.

Nutritional Information (per serving): 190 calories, 3g protein, 17g carbohydrates, 13g fat, 4g fiber, 0mg cholesterol, 320mg sodium, 740mg potassium.

ITALIAN MINESTRONE SOUP

INGREDIENTS

- 1 tablespoon olive oil
- 1/2 onion, diced. 2 cloves garlic, minced
- 1 carrot, diced
- 1 celery stalk, diced
- 1/2 zucchini, diced
- 1/2 cup canned diced tomatoes
- 4 cups lowsodium vegetable broth
- 1/2 cup cooked white beans (cannellini beans or navy beans)
- 1/2 cup chopped green beans
- 1/2 cup chopped spinach or kale
- 1/2 teaspoon dried oregano. 1/2 teaspoon dried basil
- Salt and pepper to taste

2

10 mins

25 mins

DIRECTIONS

1. Heat olive oil over medium heat in a large pot. Add diced onion and minced garlic, and sauté until softened and fragrant.
2. Add diced carrot, celery, and zucchini to the pot and cook for a few minutes until slightly tender.
3. Stir in canned diced tomatoes, vegetable broth, cooked white beans, chopped green beans, chopped spinach or kale, dried oregano, and dried basil.
4. Bring the soup to a boil, then reduce heat to low and simmer for 15-20 minutes or until all the vegetables are tender.
5. Season the minestrone with salt and pepper to taste.
6. Serve the Italian Minestrone Soup hot, garnished with grated Parmesan cheese if desired.

Nutritional Information (per serving): 212 calories, 8g protein, 32g carbohydrates, 6g fat, 8g fiber, 0mg cholesterol, 690mg sodium, 854mg potassium.

TURKISH RED LENTIL SOUP

INGREDIENTS

2

10 mins

25 mins

- 1/2 cup red lentils, rinsed and drained
- 1 tablespoon olive oil
- 1/2 onion, chopped
- 1 carrot, diced
- 1 celery stalk, diced
- 2 cloves garlic, minced
- 4 cups lowsodium vegetable broth
- 1 teaspoon ground cumin
- 1/2 teaspoon paprika. Salt and pepper to taste
- Juice of 1/2 lemon
- Fresh parsley for garnish

DIRECTIONS

1. Heat olive oil over medium heat in a large pot. Add chopped onion, diced carrot, diced celery, and minced garlic. Simmer until the vegetables soften.
2. Add rinsed red lentils to the pot and stir.
3. Pour the low sodium vegetable broth into a pot and add ground cumin, paprika, salt, and pepper. Bring to a boil.
4. Reduce heat to low, cover the pot, and simmer for about 20 minutes or until the lentils are tender.
5. Use an immersion blender or transfer the soup to a blender in batches to puree until smooth and creamy.
6. Stir in the lemon juice and adjust the seasoning if needed.
7. Serve hot, garnished with fresh parsley.

Nutritional Information (per serving): 239 calories, 12g protein, 38g carbohydrates, 5g fat, 11g fiber, 0mg cholesterol, 690mg sodium, 588mg potassium.

MOROCCAN HARIRA SOUP

INGREDIENTS

- 1/2 cup dried chickpeas, soaked overnight and drained
- 1/2 cup dried lentils, rinsed and drained
- 1 tablespoon olive oil
- 1 onion, chopped. 2 cloves garlic, minced
- 1 carrot, diced
- 1 celery stalk, diced
- 1/2 teaspoon ground cumin, coriander, turmeric, cinnamon
- 1/4 teaspoon ground ginger
- 4 cups lowsodium vegetable broth
- 1 can (15 oz) diced tomatoes
- Salt and pepper to taste
- Juice of 1/2 lemon

2

15 mins

35 mins

DIRECTIONS

1. Heat olive oil over medium heat in a large pot. Add chopped onion, minced garlic, diced carrot, and diced celery. Simmer until the vegetables soften.

2. Add soaked and drained chickpeas, rinsed and drained lentils, ground cumin, coriander, turmeric, cinnamon, and ginger to the pot. Stir to coat the vegetables and spices.

3. Add the lowsodium vegetable broth and diced tomatoes. Bring to a boil, then reduce heat to low and simmer for about 30 minutes or until the chickpeas and lentils are tender.

4. Season the soup with salt and pepper to taste. Add lemon juice.

5. Use an immersion blender or transfer a portion of the soup to a blender and whip up until the desired consistency is reached. Be careful as the soup will be hot.

6. Serve the Moroccan Harira Soup hot, garnished with fresh cilantro or parsley.

Nutritional Information (per serving): 368 calories, 17g protein, 62g carbohydrates, 7g fat, 17g fiber, 0mg cholesterol, 730mg sodium, 950mg potassium.

MEDITERRANEAN FRENCH PISTOU SOUP

INGREDIENTS

2

20 mins

20 mins

- 2 tablespoons olive oil
- 1/2 onion, chopped
- 2 cloves garlic, minced
- 2 medium tomatoes, diced
- 1 medium zucchini, diced
- 1 carrot, peeled and diced
- 4 cups vegetable broth
- 1/2 cup small pasta (such as ditalini or small shells)
- Salt and pepper to taste
- 1/4 cup grated Parmesan cheese
- 1/4 cup fresh basil leaves, chopped

DIRECTIONS

1. Heat olive oil over medium heat in a large pot. Add the chopped onion and garlic, and sauté until translucent.

2. Add the diced tomatoes, zucchini, and carrots to the pot. Cook for about 5 minutes until vegetables start to soften.

3. Pour the vegetable broth and bring the soup to a simmer. Add the small pasta and cook according to package instructions until pasta is al dente.

4. Season the soup with salt and pepper to taste. Stir in the grated Parmesan cheese and fresh basil leaves. If using cooked white beans, add them to the soup at this stage.

5. Remove the soup from heat and let it rest for a few minutes before serving.

Nutritional Information (per serving): 270 calories, 8g protein, 32g carbohydrates, 12g fat, 4g fiber, 5mg cholesterol, 1050mg sodium, 660mg potassium.

MEDITERRANEAN EGYPTIAN LENTIL SOUP

INGREDIENTS

- 1 tablespoon olive oil
- 1/2 onion, chopped
- 2 cloves garlic, minced
- 1 carrot, peeled and diced
- 1 celery stalk, diced
- 1 cup dried lentils, rinsed and drained
- 4 cups vegetable broth
- 1 teaspoon ground cumin
- 1/2 teaspoon ground coriander
- Salt and pepper to taste
- Juice of 1/2 lemon
- Fresh parsley or cilantro for garnish

2

10 mins

25 mins

DIRECTIONS

1. Heat olive oil over medium heat in a large pot. Add the chopped onion and garlic and sauté until softened and fragrant.

2. Add the diced carrot and celery to the pot and cook for a few minutes until they soften.

3. Pour the vegetable broth into a bowl and add the rinsed lentils, ground cumin, coriander, salt, and pepper. Stir well to combine.

4. Bring the soup to a boil, then reduce heat and simmer uncovered for about 20-25 minutes or until lentils are tender.

5. Remove the soup from the heat and stir in the lemon juice. Taste and adjust seasoning if needed. Serve hot, garnished with fresh parsley or cilantro.

Nutritional Information (per serving): 320 calories, 18g protein, 50g carbohydrates, 6g fat, 16g fiber, 0mg cholesterol, 780mg sodium, 1230mg potassium.

MEDITERRANEAN ISRAELI MATZO BALL SOUP

INGREDIENTS

For Matzo Balls:
- 1/2 cup matzo meal
- 2 large eggs
- 2 tablespoons olive oil
- 1/4 teaspoon salt, 1/4 black pepper
- 2 tablespoons chopped fresh parsley

For Soup:
- 4 cups chicken or vegetable broth
- 1 carrot, peeled and sliced
- 1 celery stalk, sliced
- 1/2 onion, chopped, Salt and pepper to taste

2

15 mins

25 mins

DIRECTIONS

1. Combine matzo meal, eggs, olive oil, salt, pepper, and chopped parsley in a mixing bowl. Mix until well combined. Cover the bowl and refrigerate for at least 15 minutes.

2. Bring the chicken or vegetable broth to a simmer in a large pot. Add the sliced carrot, celery, and chopped onion. Season with salt and pepper to taste.

3. Take the matzo ball mixture out of the refrigerator and shape it into small balls using your hands. Drop the matzo balls into the simmering broth.

4. Cover the pot and cook the matzo balls in the broth for about 20-25 minutes until tender.

5. Once the matzo balls are cooked, ladle the soup into serving bowls, including some vegetables and matzo balls in each bowl. Garnish with fresh dill or parsley before serving.

Nutritional Information (per serving): 300 calories, 11g protein, 38g carbohydrates, 11g fat, 3g fiber, 160mg cholesterol, 1480mg sodium, 400mg potassium.

CREAMY WILD RICE & MUSHROOM SOUP

INGREDIENTS

- 1/2 cup wild rice
- 1 tablespoon olive oil
- 1/2 onion, chopped
- 2 garlic cloves, minced
- 8 ounces cremini mushrooms, sliced
- 2 cups vegetable broth
- 1/2 cup unsweetened almond milk
- 1/4 teaspoon dried thyme
- Salt and pepper to taste
- Fresh parsley for garnish

2

10 mins

25 mins

DIRECTIONS

1. Rinse the wild rice under cold water. In a medium saucepan, bring 1 cup of water to a boil and add the wild rice. Reduce heat, cover, and simmer for 15-20 minutes until the rice is tender. Drain any excess water and set aside.

2. Heat olive oil over medium heat in a large pot. Add chopped onion and garlic, and sauté until fragrant and translucent.

3. Add sliced mushrooms to the pot and cook until they release moisture and start to brown, about 5-7 min.

4. Pour the vegetable broth and almond milk into the pot, then add the cooked wild rice and dried thyme—season with salt and pepper to taste. Bring to a simmer and cook for an additional 10 minutes.

5. Blend the soup until smooth and creamy using an immersion or a regular blender. Adjust seasoning if needed. Serve hot, garnished with fresh parsley.

Nutritional Information (per serving): 320 calories, 18g protein, 50g carbohydrates, 6g fat, 16g fiber, 0mg cholesterol, 780mg sodium, 1230mg potassium.

CREAM OF PUMPKIN SOUP

INGREDIENTS

2

15 mins

25 mins

- 1 cup pumpkin puree
- 1 tablespoon olive oil
- 1/2 onion, chopped
- 1 garlic clove, minced
- 2 cups vegetable broth
- 1/2 cup unsweetened almond milk
- 1/4 teaspoon ground cinnamon
- Salt and pepper to taste
- Pumpkin seeds for garnish (optional)

DIRECTIONS

1. Heat olive oil over medium heat in a large pot. Add chopped onion and garlic, and sauté until softened and aromatic.

2. Add the pumpkin puree to the pot and stir well to combine with the onions and garlic.

3. Pour in the vegetable broth and almond milk. Add ground cinnamon, salt, and pepper. Bring to a simmer and cook for about 15 minutes, stirring occasionally.

4. Blend the soup until smooth and creamy using an immersion or a regular blender.

5. Serve hot, garnished with a sprinkle of ground cinnamon and pumpkin seeds if desired.

Nutritional Information (per serving): 180 calories, 4g protein, 20g carbohydrates, 10g fat, 5g fiber, 0mg cholesterol, 820mg sodium, 540mg potassium.

CREAM OF ASPARAGUS SOUP

INGREDIENTS

2

10 mins

20 mins

- 1 bunch asparagus, trimmed and chopped
- 1 tablespoon olive oil
- 1/2 onion, chopped
- 1 garlic clove, minced
- 2 cups vegetable broth
- 1/2 cup unsweetened almond milk
- Salt and pepper to taste
- Fresh lemon juice for garnish
- Chopped fresh parsley for garnish

DIRECTIONS

1. Heat olive oil over medium heat in a large pot. Add chopped onion and garlic, and sauté until soft and fragrant.

2. Add chopped asparagus to the pot and cook for about 5 minutes until slightly tender.

3. Pour in the vegetable broth and bring to a simmer. Cook for 10-15 minutes until the asparagus is fully tender.

4. Blend the soup until smooth using an immersion blender or a regular blender. Stir in the almond milk and season with salt and pepper to taste.

5. Simmer for a few more minutes until heated through. Serve hot, garnished with a squeeze of fresh lemon juice and chopped parsley.

Nutritional Information (per serving): 160 calories, 6g protein, 14g carbohydrates, 10g fat, 5g fiber, 0mg cholesterol, 720mg sodium, 560mg potassium.

ROASTED TOMATO BASIL SOUP

INGREDIENTS

2

15 mins

40 mins

- 1 pound Roma tomatoes, halved
- 2 tablespoons olive oil
- Salt and pepper to taste
- 1/2 onion, chopped
- 2 garlic cloves, minced
- 2 cups vegetable broth
- 1/4 cup fresh basil leaves, chopped
- 1/2 cup unsweetened almond milk
- Optional: grated Parmesan cheese for garnish

DIRECTIONS

1. Preheat the oven to 400°F (200°C). Place the halved Roma tomatoes on a baking sheet, drizzle with olive oil, and season with salt and pepper. Roast in the oven for 25-30 minutes until softened and slightly charred.

2. Peat a tablespoon of olive oil over medium heat in a large pot. Add chopped onion and garlic, and sauté until translucent and fragrant.

3. Add the roasted tomatoes (including any juices from the baking sheet) to the pot. Pour in the vegetable broth and add chopped basil leaves. Bring to a simmer and cook for about 10 minutes.

4. Blend the soup using an immersion blender or a regular blender until smooth and creamy. Stir in the almond milk and simmer for an additional 5 minutes.

5. Season with more salt and pepper if needed. If desired, serve hot, garnished with fresh basil leaves and grated Parmesan cheese.

Nutritional Information (per serving): 230 calories, 4g protein, 14g carbohydrates, 18g fat, 3g fiber, 0mg cholesterol, 820mg sodium, 880mg potassium.

MEDITERRANEAN FISH SOUP

INGREDIENTS

- 8 ounces white fish fillets (such as cod or tilapia), cut into chunks
- 1 tablespoon olive oil; 1/2 onion, chopped
- 2 garlic cloves, minced
- 1/2 red bell pepper, chopped;
- 1/2 yellow bell pepper, chopped
- 1 can (14 ounces) diced tomatoes, drained
- 2 cups fish or vegetable broth
- 1 teaspoon dried oregano; Salt and pepper to taste
- Fresh parsley for garnish

2

15 mins

25 mins

DIRECTIONS

1. Heat olive oil over medium heat in a large pot. Add chopped onion and garlic, and sauté until softened and fragrant.

2. Add chopped bell peppers to the pot and cook for about 5 minutes until they soften.

3. Stir in the diced tomatoes, fish or vegetable broth, and dried oregano. Bring to a simmer and cook for 10 minutes.

4. Add the fish chunks to the soup and simmer for another 5-7 minutes until the fish is cooked and can flake easily with a fork.

5. Season with salt and pepper to taste. Serve hot, garnished with fresh parsley.

Nutritional Information (per serving): 240 calories, 24g protein, 14g carbohydrates, 9g fat, 3g fiber, 40mg cholesterol, 800mg sodium, 580mg potassium.

CHICKEN LEEK SOUP

INGREDIENTS

2

15 mins

25 mins

- 8 ounces boneless, skinless chicken breast, cut into bitesized pieces
- 1 tablespoon olive oil
- 1 leek, white and light green parts only, sliced
- 2 carrots, peeled and diced
- 2 celery stalks, diced
- 2 garlic cloves, minced
- 4 cups lowsodium chicken broth; 1 bay leaf
- Salt and pepper to taste
- Fresh parsley for garnish

DIRECTIONS

1. In a large pot, heat olive oil over medium heat. Add the sliced leek, carrots, celery, and minced garlic. Sauté until vegetables are tender, about 5-7 minutes.

2. Add the chicken breast pieces to the pot and cook until they are no longer pink about 5 minutes.

3. Pour in the chicken broth and add the bay leaf. Bring the soup to a simmer and cook for 10-15 minutes until the chicken is cooked.

4. Season with salt and pepper to taste. Remove the bay leaf before serving.

5. Ladle the soup into bowls, garnish with fresh parsley, and serve hot.

Nutritional Information (per serving): 240 calories, 28g protein, 12g carbohydrates, 9g fat, 3g fiber, 70mg cholesterol, 560mg sodium, 700mg potassium.

WHITE BEAN SOUP

INGREDIENTS

- 1 can (15 ounces) white beans, drained and rinsed
- 1 tablespoon olive oil
- 1/2 onion, chopped
- 2 garlic cloves, minced
- 2 cups lowsodium vegetable broth
- 1/2 teaspoon dried thyme
- Salt and pepper to taste
- Fresh parsley for garnish

2

10 mins

30 mins

DIRECTIONS

1. Heat olive oil over medium heat in a large pot. Add the chopped onion and Heat olive oil over medium heat in a large pot. Add chopped onion and garlic, and sauté until softened and fragrant.

2. Add the drained and rinsed white beans to the pot. Stir well to combine with the onion and garlic.

3. Pour in the vegetable broth and add dried thyme. Bring the soup to a simmer and cook for 15-20 minutes to allow the flavors to meld together.

4. Blend the soup until smooth and creamy using an immersion or a regular blender. Alternatively, you can leave it slightly chunky if desired.

5. Season with salt and pepper to taste. Serve hot, garnished with fresh parsley.

Nutritional Information (per serving): 220 calories, 9g protein, 32g carbohydrates, 7g fat, 8g fiber, 0mg cholesterol, 500mg sodium, 770mg potassium.

GREEK SALAD

INGREDIENTS

- 1 large cucumber, diced
- 1 cup cherry tomatoes, halved
- 1/2 red onion, thinly sliced; 1/2 green bell pepper, diced
- 1/4 cup Kalamata olives, pitted and sliced
- 2 ounces feta cheese, crumbled
- 2 tablespoons extra virgin olive oil
- 1 tablespoon red wine vinegar
- 1 teaspoon dried oregano
- Salt and pepper to taste; Fresh parsley for garnish

2

15 mins

0 mins

DIRECTIONS

1. In a large bowl, combine diced cucumber, halved cherry tomatoes, thinly sliced red onion, diced green bell pepper, sliced Kalamata olives, and crumbled feta cheese.

2. To make the dressing, whisk together extra virgin olive oil, red wine vinegar, dried oregano, salt, and pepper in a small bowl.

3. Pour the dressing over the salad ingredients in a large bowl. Toss well to coat all the vegetables and cheese evenly with the dressing.

4. Taste and adjust seasoning if needed. Serve the Greek salad chilled or at room temperature, garnished with fresh parsley.

Nutritional Information (per serving): 280 calories, 9g protein, 15g carbohydrates, 21g fat, 5g fiber, 20mg cholesterol, 560mg sodium, 620mg potassium.

MEDITERRANEAN CHICKPEA SALAD

INGREDIENTS

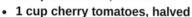

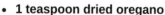

2

10 mins

0 mins

- 1 can (15 ounces) chickpeas, drained and rinsed
- 1 cup cucumber, diced
- 1 cup cherry tomatoes, halved
- 1/4 red onion, thinly sliced
- 1/4 cup Kalamata olives, pitted and sliced
- 2 tablespoons extra virgin olive oil
- 1 tablespoon lemon juice
- 1 teaspoon dried oregano
- Salt and pepper to taste
- Fresh parsley for garnish

DIRECTIONS

1. Combine the drained and rinsed chickpeas, diced cucumber, halved cherry tomatoes, thinly sliced red onion, and sliced Kalamata olives in a large bowl.

2. To make the dressing, whisk together extra virgin olive oil, lemon juice, dried oregano, salt, and pepper in a small bowl.

3. In a large bowl, pour the dressing over the chickpea salad ingredients. Toss well to coat all the vegetables and chickpeas evenly with the dressing.

4. Taste and adjust seasoning if needed. Serve the Mediterranean chickpea salad chilled or at room temperature, garnished with fresh parsley.

Nutritional Information (per serving): 320 calories, 9g protein, 32g carbohydrates, 18g fat, 8g fiber, 0mg cholesterol, 680mg sodium, 660mg potassium.

QUINOA TABBOULEH SALAD

INGREDIENTS

- 1/2 cup quinoa
- 1 cup water; 1 cup cucumber, diced
- 1 cup cherry tomatoes, halved
- 1/2 cup fresh parsley, chopped
- 1/4 cup fresh mint leaves, chopped
- 1/4 cup red onion, finely chopped
- 2 tablespoons extra virgin olive oil
- 2 tablespoons lemon juice
- Salt and pepper to taste

2

15 mins

15 mins

DIRECTIONS

1. Rinse the quinoa under cold water. Combine the quinoa and water in a saucepan. Bring to a boil, then reduce heat to low, cover, and simmer for 12-15 minutes until the quinoa is cooked and the water is absorbed. Remove from heat and let it cool.
2. Combine the cooked quinoa, diced cucumber, halved cherry tomatoes, chopped parsley, chopped mint leaves, and finely chopped red onion in a large bowl.
3. To make the dressing, whisk together extra virgin olive oil, lemon juice, salt, and pepper in a small bowl.
4. Pour the dressing over the quinoa tabbouleh salad ingredients in a large bowl. Toss well to coat everything evenly with the dressing.
5. Taste and adjust seasoning if needed. Serve the quinoa tabbouleh salad chilled or at room temperature.

Nutritional Information (per serving): 290 calories, 7g protein, 35g carbohydrates, 14g fat, 5g fiber, 0mg cholesterol, 220mg sodium, 430mg potassium.

CAPRESE SALAD

INGREDIENTS

2

10 mins

0 mins

- 1 large tomato, sliced
- 4 ounces fresh mozzarella cheese, sliced
- Fresh basil leaves
- 1 tablespoon extra virgin olive oil
- 1 tablespoon balsamic glaze
- Salt and pepper to taste

DIRECTIONS

1. Arrange the sliced tomato and fresh mozzarella cheese alternately on a serving plate.
2. Tuck fresh basil leaves in between the tomato and cheese slices.
3. Drizzle extra virgin olive oil and balsamic glaze over the salad.
4. Season with salt and pepper to taste.
5. Serve the Caprese salad immediately as a refreshing appetizer or side dish.

Nutritional Information (per serving): 260 calories, 14g protein, 4g carbohydrates, 20g fat, 1g fiber, 45mg cholesterol, 430mg sodium, 300mg potassium.

TUNA AND WHITE BEAN SALAD

INGREDIENTS

- 1 can (5 ounces) tuna, drained
- 1 can (15 ounces) white beans, drained and rinsed
- 1/2 red onion, finely chopped
- 1/2 red bell pepper, diced
- 1/4 cup Kalamata olives, pitted and sliced
- 2 tablespoons extra virgin olive oil
- 1 tablespoon lemon juice
- 1 teaspoon Dijon mustard
- Salt and pepper to taste
- Fresh parsley for garnish

2

10 mins

0 mins

DIRECTIONS

1. Combine the drained tuna, white beans, finely chopped red onion, diced red bell pepper, and sliced Kalamata olives in a large bowl.

2. To make the dressing, whisk together extra virgin olive oil, lemon juice, Dijon mustard, salt, and pepper in a small bowl.

3. In a large bowl, pour the dressing over the tuna and white bean salad ingredients. Toss well to coat everything evenly with the dressing.

4. Taste and adjust seasoning if needed. Serve the tuna and white bean salad chilled or at room temperature, garnished with fresh parsley.

Nutritional Information (per serving): 380 calories, 30g protein, 30g carbohydrates, 15g fat, 8g fiber, 30mg cholesterol, 590mg sodium, 980mg potassium.

MEDITERRANEAN CUCUMBER SALAD

INGREDIENTS

2

10 mins

0 mins

- 1 large cucumber, thinly sliced
- 1/2 red onion, thinly sliced
- 1/2 cup cherry tomatoes, halved
- 1/4 cup Kalamata olives, pitted and sliced
- 2 tablespoons extra virgin olive oil
- 1 tablespoon red wine vinegar
- 1 teaspoon dried oregano
- Salt and pepper to taste
- Crumbled feta cheese for garnish (optional)

DIRECTIONS

1. In a large bowl, combine the thinly sliced cucumber, thinly sliced red onion, halved cherry tomatoes, and sliced Kalamata olives.

2. To make the dressing, whisk together extra virgin olive oil, red wine vinegar, dried oregano, salt, and pepper in a small bowl.

3. Pour the dressing over the cucumber salad ingredients in a large bowl. Toss well to coat everything evenly with the dressing.

4. Taste and adjust seasoning if needed. Serve the Mediterranean cucumber salad chilled or at room temperature, garnished with crumbled feta cheese if desired.

Nutritional Information (per serving): 180 calories, 2g protein, 10g carbohydrates, 15g fat, 2g fiber, 0mg cholesterol, 230mg sodium, 350mg potassium.

MEDITERRANEAN LENTIL SALAD

INGREDIENTS

- 1/2 cup dry lentils
- 1 cup water
- 1/2 cucumber, diced
- 1/2 red bell pepper, diced
- 1/4 red onion, finely chopped
- 1/4 cup Kalamata olives, pitted and sliced
- 2 tablespoons extra virgin olive oil
- 1 tablespoon red wine vinegar
- 1 teaspoon dried oregano
- Salt and pepper to taste
- Crumbled feta cheese for garnish (optional)

2

10 mins

20 mins

DIRECTIONS

1. Rinse the dry lentils under cold water. Combine the lentils and water in a saucepan. Bring to a boil, then reduce heat to low, cover, and simmer for 15-20 minutes until tender. Drain any excess water and let the lentils cool.

2. Combine the cooked lentils, diced cucumber, red bell pepper, finely chopped red onion, and sliced Kalamata olives in a large bowl.

3. To make the dressing, whisk together extra virgin olive oil, red wine vinegar, dried oregano, salt, and pepper in a small bowl.

4. Pour the dressing over the lentil salad ingredients in a large bowl. Toss well to coat everything evenly with the dressing.

5. Taste and adjust seasoning if needed. Serve the Mediterranean lentil salad chilled or at room temperature, garnished with crumbled feta cheese if desired.

Nutritional Information (per serving): 320 calories, 15g protein, 35g carbohydrates, 14g fat, 12g fiber, 0mg cholesterol, 220mg sodium, 660mg potassium.

MEDITERRANEAN BEET SALAD

INGREDIENTS

2

15 mins

45 mins

- 2 medium beets, peeled and diced
- 1 tablespoon extra virgin olive oil
- Salt and pepper to taste
- 1/2 cup cooked chickpeas, drained and rinsed
- 1/4 cup crumbled feta cheese
- 2 tablespoons chopped fresh parsley
- 2 tablespoons chopped fresh mint
- 1 tablespoon lemon juice
- 1 tablespoon balsamic vinegar
- 1 tablespoon honey (optional for sweetness)
- 2 cups mixed greens

DIRECTIONS

1. Preheat the oven to 400°F (200°C). Place the diced beets on a baking sheet, drizzle with olive oil, and season with salt and pepper. Roast in the oven for 40-45 minutes until the beets are tender and slightly caramelized. Let them cool.

2. In a large bowl, combine the roasted beets, cooked chickpeas, crumbled feta cheese, chopped parsley, and chopped mint.

3. To make the dressing, whisk together lemon juice, balsamic vinegar, honey (if using), salt, and pepper in a small bowl.

4. Pour the dressing over the beet salad ingredients in a large bowl. Toss well to coat everything evenly with the dressing.

5. To serve, divide the mixed greens between two plates and top with the Mediterranean beet salad mixture.

Nutritional Information (per serving): 280 calories, 8g protein, 40g carbohydrates, 11g fat, 9g fiber, 10mg cholesterol, 480mg sodium, 980mg potassium.

MEDITERRANEAN COUSCOUS SALAD

INGREDIENTS

2

15 mins

10 mins

- 1/2 cup dry couscous
- 3/4 cup water or vegetable broth
- 1/2 cucumber, diced
- 1/2 red bell pepper, diced
- 1/4 red onion, finely chopped
- 1/4 cup Kalamata olives, pitted and sliced
- 2 tablespoons extra virgin olive oil
- 1 tablespoon lemon juice
- 1 teaspoon dried oregano
- Salt and pepper to taste
- Crumbled feta cheese for garnish (optional)
- Fresh parsley for garnish

DIRECTIONS

1. In a saucepan, bring water or vegetable broth to a boil. Stir in the dry couscous, cover, and remove from heat. Let it sit for about 5 minutes until the couscous absorbs the liquid—fluff with a fork.
2. In a large bowl, combine the cooked couscous, diced cucumber, red bell pepper, finely chopped red onion, and sliced Kalamata olives.
3. In a small bowl, whisk together extra virgin olive oil, lemon juice, dried oregano, salt, and pepper to make the dressing.
4. Pour the dressing over the couscous salad ingredients in the large bowl. Toss well to coat everything evenly with the dressing.
5. Taste and adjust seasoning if needed. Serve the Mediterranean couscous salad chilled or at room temperature, garnished with crumbled feta cheese and fresh parsley if desired.

Nutritional Information (per serving): 290 calories, 7g protein, 40g carbohydrates, 11g fat, 5g fiber, 0mg cholesterol, 230mg sodium, 320mg potassium.

MOROCCAN CARROT SALAD

INGREDIENTS

2

15 mins

0 mins

- 2 large carrots, peeled and grated
- 1/4 cup raisins or dried cranberries
- 1 tablespoon fresh parsley, chopped
- 1 tablespoon fresh cilantro, chopped
- 1 tablespoon lemon juice
- 1 tablespoon extra virgin olive oil
- 1 teaspoon ground cumin
- 1/2 teaspoon ground cinnamon
- 1/4 teaspoon ground coriander
- Salt and pepper to taste
- 1 tablespoon slivered almonds or toasted pine nuts (optional)

DIRECTIONS

1. In a large bowl, combine the grated carrots, raisins, fresh parsley, and fresh cilantro.
2. In a small bowl, whisk together the lemon juice, extra virgin olive oil, ground cumin, cinnamon, coriander, salt, and pepper.
3. Pour the dressing over the carrot mixture, and toss until the salad is evenly coated with the dressing.
4. Taste and adjust the seasoning as needed. Garnish with slivered almonds or toasted pine nuts, if desired. Serve the Moroccan carrot salad chilled or at room temperature.

Nutritional Information (per serving): 160 calories, 2g protein, 21g carbohydrates, 9g fat, 5g fiber, 0mg cholesterol, 160mg sodium, 300mg potassium.

SHRIMP, ARUGULA, AND AVOCADO SALAD

INGREDIENTS

- 8 ounces shrimp, peeled and deveined
- 2 cups arugula
- 1 avocado, sliced
- 1/2 cup cherry tomatoes, halved
- 1/4 red onion, thinly sliced
- 2 tablespoons extra virgin olive oil
- 1 tablespoon lemon juice
- Salt and pepper to taste
- Crushed red pepper flakes (optional)
- Fresh parsley for garnish

2

15 mins

10 mins

DIRECTIONS

1. Heat a skillet over medium-high heat and add a drizzle of olive oil. Cook the shrimp on each side for 2-3 minutes until pink and cooked through. Remove from heat and set aside.
2. In a large bowl, combine arugula, sliced avocado, halved cherry tomatoes, and thinly sliced red onion.
3. Add extra virgin olive oil, lemon juice, salt, and pepper in a small bowl to make the dressing. If desired, add crushed red pepper flakes for a bit of heat.
4. Pour the dressing over the salad ingredients in a large bowl. Toss well to coat everything evenly with the dressing.
5. Divide the salad between two plates, top with cooked shrimp, and garnish with fresh parsley.

Nutritional Information (per serving): 320 calories, 25g protein, 15g carbohydrates, 20g fat, 6g fiber, 150mg cholesterol, 350mg sodium, 820mg potassium

SARDINE SALAD

INGREDIENTS

2

10 mins

0 mins

- 1 can (25 ounces) of sardines in olive oil, drained
- 2 cups mixed salad greens
- 1/2 cucumber, sliced
- 1/2 cup cherry tomatoes, halved
- 1/4 red onion, thinly sliced
- 2 tablespoons extra virgin olive oil
- 1 tablespoon lemon juice
- Salt and pepper to taste
- Fresh parsley for garnish

DIRECTIONS

1. combine mixed salad greens, sliced cucumber, halved cherry tomatoes, and thinly sliced red onion in a large bowl.
2. Open the sardine can and drain the excess olive oil. Add the sardines to the salad bowl.
3. Adda virgin olive oil, lemon juice, salt, and pepper to a small bowl to make the dressing4. Pour the dressing over the salad ingredients in a large bowl. Toss well to coat everything evenly with the dressing.
5. Divide the sardine salad between two plates, garnish with fresh parsley, and serve immediately.

Nutritional Information (per serving): 310 calories, 20g protein, 10g carbohydrates, 24g fat, 3g fiber, 55mg cholesterol, 420mg sodium, 530mg potassium.

ROASTED VEGETABLES

INGREDIENTS

- 1 medium zucchini, sliced
- 1 medium yellow squash, sliced
- 1 red bell pepper, sliced
- 1 yellow bell pepper, sliced
- 1 small red onion, sliced
- 2 tablespoons extra virgin olive oil
- 1 teaspoon dried oregano; 1 teaspoon dried thyme
- Salt and pepper to taste
- Fresh parsley for garnish

2

15 mins

25 mins

DIRECTIONS

1. Preheat the oven to 425°F (220°C). Line a baking sheet with parchment paper or foil for easy cleanup.
2. In a large bowl, toss the sliced zucchini, yellow squash, red bell pepper, yellow bell pepper, red onion with extra virgin olive oil, dried oregano, dried thyme, salt, and pepper until evenly coated.
3. Spread the seasoned vegetables in a single layer on the prepared baking sheet.
4. Roast the vegetables in the preheated oven for 20-25 minutes, stirring halfway through cooking, until they are tender and slightly caramelized.
5. Remove the roasted vegetables from the oven and transfer them to a serving dish. Garnish with fresh parsley before serving.

Nutritional Information (per serving): 180 calories, 3g protein, 15g carbohydrates, 12g fat, 5g fiber, 0mg cholesterol, 10mg sodium, 600mg potassium.

QUINOA TABBOULEH

INGREDIENTS

2

15 mins

15 mins

- 1/2 cup quinoa
- 1 cup water or vegetable broth
- 1/2 cup fresh parsley, chopped
- 1/4 cup fresh mint leaves, chopped
- 1/2 cucumber, finely diced
- 1/2 cup cherry tomatoes, halved
- 1/4 red onion, finely chopped
- 2 tablespoons extra virgin olive oil
- 2 tablespoons lemon juice
- Salt and pepper to taste

DIRECTIONS

1. Rinse the quinoa under cold water. Combine the quinoa and water or vegetable broth in a saucepan. Bring to a boil, then reduce heat, cover, and simmer for about 12-15 minutes until the liquid is absorbed and the quinoa is tender. Fluff with a fork and let it cool.
2. In a large bowl, combine the cooked quinoa, chopped parsley, chopped mint leaves, finely diced cucumber, halved cherry tomatoes, and red onion.
3. To make the dressing, whisk together extra virgin olive oil, lemon juice, salt, and pepper in a small bowl.
4. Pour the dressing over the quinoa tabbouleh ingredients in the large bowl. Toss well to coat everything evenly with the dressing.
5. Taste and adjust seasoning if needed. Serve the quinoa tabbouleh chilled or at room temperature.

Nutritional Information (per serving): 320 calories, 8g protein, 40g carbohydrates, 15g fat, 6g fiber, 0mg cholesterol, 220mg sodium, 470mg potassium.

SAUTÉED SPINACH WITH GARLIC

INGREDIENTS

- 1 tablespoon olive oil
- 2 cloves garlic, minced
- 6 cups fresh spinach leaves
- Salt and pepper to taste
- Lemon wedges for serving (optional)

2

5 mins

5 mins

DIRECTIONS

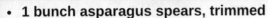

1. Heat olive oil in a large skillet over medium heat.

2. Add minced garlic to the skillet and sauté for about 1 minute until fragrant.

3. Add fresh spinach leaves to the skillet and toss them with the garlic and oil until wilted, about 2-3 minutes.

4. Season the spinach with salt and pepper to taste.

5. Remove the sautéed spinach from the heat and transfer it to serving plates. If desired, serve with lemon wedges on the side.

Nutritional Information (per serving): 80 calories, 4g protein, 6g carbohydrates, 5g fat, 3g fiber, 0mg cholesterol, 150mg sodium, 800mg potassium.

GRILLED ASPARAGUS

INGREDIENTS

2

5 mins

10 mins

- 1 bunch asparagus spears, trimmed
- 1 tablespoon olive oil
- Salt and pepper to taste
- Lemon wedges for serving (optional)

DIRECTIONS

1. Preheat the grill to medium-high heat.

2. Drizzle olive oil over the trimmed asparagus spears and toss to coat them evenly.

3. Season the asparagus with salt and pepper to taste.

4. Place the asparagus spears on the preheated grill and cook for about 8-10 minutes, turning occasionally, until they are tender and slightly charred.

5. Remove the grilled asparagus and transfer it to a serving platter. If desired, serve with lemon wedges on the side.

Nutritional Information (per serving): 80 calories, 4g protein, 6g carbohydrates, 5g fat, 3g fiber, 0mg cholesterol, 0mg sodium, 500mg potassium.

COUSCOUS WITH LEMON AND HERBS

INGREDIENTS

2

10 mins

10 mins

- 1/2 cup couscous
- 3/4 cup water or vegetable broth
- 1 tablespoon olive oil
- Zest of 1 lemon
- 2 tablespoons fresh lemon juice
- 2 tablespoons chopped fresh herbs (such as parsley, cilantro, or mint)
- Salt and pepper to taste

DIRECTIONS

1. Bring the water or vegetable broth to a boil in a small saucepan.
2. Stir in the couscous, cover the saucepan, and remove it from heat. Let it sit for about 5 minutes to allow the couscous to absorb the liquid.
3. Fluff the cooked couscous with a fork to separate the grains.
4. In a bowl, combine the cooked couscous, olive oil, lemon zest, fresh lemon juice, chopped fresh herbs, salt, and pepper. Mix well to combine all the flavors.
5. Taste and adjust seasoning if needed. Serve the couscous with lemon and herbs as a side dish or a light main course.

Nutritional Information (per serving): 220 calories, 5g protein, 40g carbohydrates, 4g fat, 3g fiber, 0mg cholesterol, 300mg sodium, 100mg potassium.

MARINATED ARTICHOKES

INGREDIENTS

2

10 mins

0 mins

- 1 can (14 ounces) artichoke hearts, drained and quartered
- 2 tablespoons extra virgin olive oil
- 1 tablespoon lemon juice
- 2 cloves garlic, minced
- 1 teaspoon dried oregano
- Salt and pepper to taste
- Fresh parsley for garnish (optional)

DIRECTIONS

1. Combine the quartered artichoke hearts, extra virgin olive oil, lemon juice, minced garlic, dried oregano, salt, and pepper in a bowl. Mix well to coat the artichokes evenly with the marinade.
2. Cover the bowl with plastic wrap or a lid and refrigerate for 30 minutes to allow the flavors to meld together.
3. Before serving, gently stir the marinated artichokes to ensure they are well coated with the marinade.
4. Transfer the marinated artichokes to a serving dish and garnish with fresh parsley if desired.
5. Serve chilled or at room temperature as a flavorful appetizer or side dish.

Nutritional Information (per serving): 180 calories, 2g protein, 10g carbohydrates, 15g fat, 4g fiber, 0mg cholesterol, 450mg sodium, 250mg potassium.

HUMMUS

INGREDIENTS

- 1 can (15 ounces) chickpeas, drained and rinsed
- 2 tablespoons tahini
- 2 tablespoons extra virgin olive oil
- 2 tablespoons lemon juice
- 1 clove garlic, minced
- 1/2 teaspoon ground cumin
- Salt to taste
- Water (as needed for desired consistency)

2

10 mins

0 mins

DIRECTIONS

1. In a food processor, combine the drained and rinsed chickpeas, tahini, extra virgin olive oil, lemon juice, minced garlic, ground cumin, and salt.
2. Blend the ingredients until smooth, scraping down the sides of the food processor as needed.
3. If the hummus is too thick, add water, one tablespoon at a time, until you reach your desired creamy consistency.
4. Taste the hummus and adjust the seasoning if needed by adding more salt or lemon juice.
5. Transfer the hummus to a serving bowl, drizzle with some extra olive oil, and sprinkle with a pinch of cumin or paprika for garnish if desired.

Nutritional Information (per serving): 180 calories, 6g protein, 12g carbohydrates, 13g fat, 4g fiber, 0mg cholesterol, 300mg sodium, 230mg potassium.

BABA GANOUSH

INGREDIENTS

2

10 mins

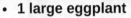

30 mins

- 1 large eggplant
- 2 tablespoons tahini
- 2 tablespoons extra virgin olive oil
- 2 cloves garlic, minced
- 2 tablespoons lemon juice
- Salt and pepper to taste
- Fresh parsley for garnish (optional)

DIRECTIONS

1. Preheat the oven to 400°F (200°C). Prick the eggplant several times with a fork and place it on a baking sheet lined with parchment paper.
2. Roast the eggplant in the preheated oven for 25-30 minutes or until the skin is charred and the flesh is soft. Remove it from the oven and let it cool slightly.
3. Cut the roasted eggplant in half and scoop the flesh into a bowl, discarding the skin.
4. Add tahini, extra virgin olive oil, minced garlic, lemon juice, salt, and pepper to the bowl with the eggplant flesh.
5. Use a fork or a food processor to mash and blend the ingredients until smooth and well combined.
6. Taste and adjust seasoning if needed by adding more salt, pepper, or lemon juice.
7. Transfer the baba ganoush to a serving dish, garnish with fresh parsley if desired, and drizzle with some extra olive oil before serving.

Nutritional Information (per serving): 150 calories, 3g protein, 10g carbohydrates, 12g fat, 5g fiber, 0mg cholesterol, 150mg sodium, 350mg potassium.

STUFFED BELL PEPPERS

INGREDIENTS

- 2 large bell peppers
- 1/2 cup cooked quinoa
- 1/2 cup canned chickpeas, drained and rinsed
- 1/4 cup diced tomatoes; 1/4 cup diced cucumber
- 1/4 cup chopped fresh parsley; 1/4 cup crumbled feta cheese
- 1 tablespoon olive oil
- 1 teaspoon lemon juice; 1 teaspoon dried oregano
- Salt and pepper to taste
- Optional: pinch of red pepper flakes

2

15 mins

35 mins

DIRECTIONS

1. Preheat the oven to 375°F (190°C). Cut the tops off the bell peppers and remove the seeds and membranes.

2. In a bowl, mix the cooked quinoa, chickpeas, diced tomatoes, diced cucumber, chopped parsley, crumbled feta cheese, olive oil, lemon juice, dried oregano, salt, pepper, and red pepper flakes if using.

3. Stuff the bell peppers with the quinoa mixture, pressing it down gently to fill them evenly.

4. Cover the stuffed bell peppers in a baking dish with foil.

5. Bake in the oven for about 30 minutes, then remove the foil and bake for 5 minutes or until the peppers are tender and the filling is heated.

6. Remove from the oven and let the stuffed peppers cool slightly before serving.

Nutritional Information (per serving): 350 calories, 12g protein, 45g carbohydrates, 15g fat, 10g fiber, 10mg cholesterol, 500mg sodium, 800mg potassium.

SPINACH AND FETA STUFFED PORTOBELLO MUSHROOMS

INGREDIENTS

2

15 mins

20 mins

- 2 large Portobello mushrooms
- 2 cups fresh spinach, chopped
- 1/2 cup crumbled feta cheese
- 2 cloves garlic, minced
- 2 tablespoons olive oil
- Salt and pepper to taste
- Optional: chopped fresh herbs (such as parsley or basil)

DIRECTIONS

1. Preheat the oven to 375°F (190°C). Clean the Portobello mushrooms and remove the stems.

2. In a skillet, heat olive oil over medium heat. Add minced garlic and sauté until fragrant, about 12 minutes.

3. Add chopped spinach to the skillet and cook until wilted, stirring occasionally, about 3-4 minutes.

4. Remove the skillet from heat and stir in crumbled feta cheese. Season with salt and pepper to taste. If using fresh herbs, add them as well.

5. Place the Portobello mushrooms on a baking sheet lined with parchment paper or aluminum foil, gill side up. Divide the spinach and feta mixture evenly between the mushrooms, filling the cavities.

6. Bake in the oven for 15-20 minutes or until the mushrooms are tender and the filling is lightly browned.

7. Remove from the oven and let the stuffed mushrooms cool slightly before serving.

Nutritional Information (per serving): 80 calories, 4g protein, 6g carbohydrates, 6g fat, 3g fiber, 0mg cholesterol, 150mg sodium, 350mg potassium.

• SIDE DISHES FOR MEAT •

GRILLED VEGETABLES

INGREDIENTS

- 1 medium zucchini, sliced
- 1 medium yellow squash, sliced
- 1 red bell pepper, sliced; 1 yellow bell pepper, sliced
- 1 red onion, sliced into rings
- 2 tablespoons olive oil
- 2 cloves garlic, minced
- 1 teaspoon dried Italian seasoning
- Salt and black pepper to taste
- Fresh basil leaves for garnish (optional)

2

10 mins

15 mins

DIRECTIONS

1. Preheat the grill to medium-high heat.
2. Combine zucchini, yellow squash, red bell pepper, yellow bell pepper, red onion, olive oil, minced garlic, dried Italian seasoning, salt, and black pepper in a large bowl. Toss to coat the vegetables evenly with the seasoning and oil.
3. Thread the vegetables onto skewers or place them on the grill grate.
4. Grill the vegetables for about 5-7 minutes per side or until they are tender and have excellent grill marks.
5. Remove the grilled vegetables from the grill and garnish with fresh basil leaves if desired before serving.

Nutritional Information (per serving): 180 calories, 4g protein, 15g carbohydrates, 12g fat, 5g fiber, 0mg cholesterol, 320mg sodium, 630mg potassium.

MEDITERRANEAN KALE

INGREDIENTS

2

10 mins

15 mins

- 6 cups chopped kale
- 2 tablespoons olive oil
- 2 cloves garlic, minced
- 1/4 teaspoon red pepper flakes
- 1/4 cup chopped sundried tomatoes
- 1/4 cup sliced Kalamata olives
- Salt and black pepper to taste
- 2 tablespoons lemon juice
- 2 tablespoons crumbled feta cheese (optional)

DIRECTIONS

1. Heat olive oil over medium heat in a large skillet. Add minced garlic and red pepper flakes, sautéing until fragrant.
2. Add chopped kale to the skillet and cook until wilted, about 5-7 minutes.
3. Stir in sundried tomatoes and Kalamata olives, then season with salt and black pepper to taste.
4. Drizzle lemon juice over the kale mixture and toss everything together.
5. If using, sprinkle crumbled feta cheese on top before serving.

Nutritional Information (per serving): 195 calories, 6g protein, 16g carbohydrates, 13g fat, 3g fiber, 0mg cholesterol, 330mg sodium, 922mg potassium.

GRILLED BROCCOLI

INGREDIENTS

- 1 head of broccoli, cut into florets
- 2 tablespoons olive oil
- 2 cloves garlic, minced
- 1/2 teaspoon dried oregano
- Salt and black pepper to taste
- Lemon wedges for serving

2

5 mins

15 mins

DIRECTIONS

1. Preheat the grill to medium-high heat.
2. Toss broccoli florets with olive oil, minced garlic, dried oregano, salt, and black pepper until evenly coated.
3. Place the broccoli on the preheated grill and cook for about 10-12 minutes, turning occasionally, until tender and lightly charred.
4. Remove the grilled broccoli and squeeze fresh lemon juice over the top before serving.

Nutritional Information (per serving): 120 calories, 4g protein, 9g carbohydrates, 9g fat, 3g fiber, 0mg cholesterol, 60mg sodium, 460mg potassium.

ITALIAN GRILLED EGGPLANT

INGREDIENTS

2

10 mins

10 mins

- 1 large eggplant, sliced into 1/2inch rounds
- 2 tablespoons olive oil
- 2 cloves garlic, minced
- 1 teaspoon dried basil
- 1/2 teaspoon dried oregano
- Salt and black pepper to taste
- 1/4 cup grated Parmesan cheese
- Fresh basil leaves for garnish (optional)

DIRECTIONS

1. Preheat the grill to medium-high heat.
2. In a small bowl, mix olive oil, minced garlic, dried basil, dried oregano, salt, and black pepper to create a marinade.
3. Brush both sides of the eggplant slices with the marinade.
4. Grill the eggplant slices for 4-5 minutes per side or until tender and grill marks appear.
5. Sprinkle grated Parmesan cheese over the grilled eggplant slices and garnish with fresh basil leaves if desired before serving.

Nutritional Information (per serving): 180 calories, 5g protein, 14g carbohydrates, 13g fat, 6g fiber, 5mg cholesterol, 300mg sodium, 570mg potassium.

ZUCCHINI BOATS

INGREDIENTS

- 2 medium zucchinis
- 1/2 cup marinara sauce
- 1/2 cup shredded mozzarella cheese
- 1/4 cup grated Parmesan cheese
- 1/4 cup chopped fresh basil
- Salt and black pepper to taste
- Olive oil for drizzling

2

15 mins

25 mins

DIRECTIONS

1. Preheat the oven to 400°F (200°C).
2. Cut the zucchinis in half lengthwise and scoop out the seeds and flesh using a spoon, leaving about a 1/4-inch shell.
3. Place the zucchini halves on a lightly greased baking sheet lined with parchment paper.
4. Season the zucchini boats with salt and black pepper, then fill each vessel with marinara sauce.
5. Sprinkle shredded mozzarella cheese and grated Parmesan cheese over the marinara sauce in each zucchini boat.
6. Drizzle olive oil over the top of the zucchini boats and bake in the preheated oven for about 20-25 minutes or until the zucchini is tender and the cheese is melted and bubbly.
7. Remove the zucchini boats from the oven, sprinkle chopped fresh basil on top, and serve hot.

Nutritional Information (per serving): 195 calories, 10g protein, 12g carbohydrates, 12g fat, 3g fiber, 25mg cholesterol, 460mg sodium, 840mg potassium.

VEGETABLE BIRDSEED PILAF

INGREDIENTS

2

10 mins

25 mins

- 1/2 cup quinoa, rinsed
- 1/2 cup wild rice blend; 1 cup vegetable broth
- 1 tablespoon olive oil
- 1 small onion, finely chopped
- 1 carrot, diced; 1 celery stalk, diced
- 1/2 cup frozen peas
- 1/4 cup chopped parsley
- Salt and black pepper to taste
- Lemon wedges for serving (optional)

DIRECTIONS

1. Combine the quinoa, wild rice blend, and vegetable broth in a medium saucepan. Bring to a boil, then reduce heat to low, cover, and simmer for 15-20 minutes or until the grains are tender and the liquid is absorbed.
2. In a separate skillet, heat olive oil over medium heat. Add chopped onion, diced carrot, and diced celery. Sauté until the vegetables are tender, about 5-7 minutes.
3. Add frozen peas to the skillet and cook for 2-3 minutes until heated.
4. Fluff the cooked quinoa and wild rice with a fork, then stir in the sautéed vegetables and chopped parsley—season with salt and black pepper to taste.
5. Serve the vegetable birdseed pilaf hot, optionally garnished with lemon wedges.

Nutritional Information (per serving): 290 calories, 9g protein, 47g carbohydrates, 8g fat, 7g fiber, 0mg cholesterol, 480mg sodium, 540mg potassium.

GREEK LEMON POTATOES

INGREDIENTS

- 2 medium russet potatoes, peeled and cut into wedges
- 2 tablespoons olive oil
- 2 tablespoons lemon juice (freshly squeezed)
- 2 cloves garlic, minced
- 1 teaspoon dried oregano
- 1/2 teaspoon salt
- 1/4 teaspoon black pepper
- 1/4 cup chicken or vegetable broth
- Fresh parsley for garnish (optional)

2

10 mins

40 mins

DIRECTIONS

1. Preheat the oven to 400°F (200°C).
2. In a large bowl, combine olive oil, lemon juice, minced garlic, oregano, salt, and pepper. Whisk together until well blended.
3. Add the potato wedges to the bowl and toss to coat them evenly with the lemon and olive oil mixture.
4. Arrange the potatoes in a single layer on a baking dish and pour the broth around them.
5. Roast the potatoes for 35-40 minutes, flipping them halfway through, until they are golden brown and tender.
6. Remove from the oven and garnish with freshly chopped parsley if desired before serving.

Nutritional Information (per serving): 220 calories, 3g protein, 28g carbohydrates, 11g fat, 3g fiber, 0mg cholesterol, 320mg sodium, 500mg potassium.

BAKED SWEET POTATOES

INGREDIENTS

2

10 mins

45 mins

- 2 medium sweet potatoes
- 1 tablespoon olive oil; 1 teaspoon ground cumin
- 1/2 teaspoon smoked paprika; 1/4 teaspoon garlic powder
- Salt and black pepper to taste
- 1/4 cup crumbled feta cheese
- 1/4 cup cherry tomatoes, chopped
- 2 tablespoons kalamata olives, chopped
- 1 tablespoon fresh parsley, chopped
- 2 tablespoons plain Greek yogurt (optional)

DIRECTIONS

1. Preheat the oven to 400°F (200°C).
2. Wash and scrub the sweet potatoes, then pat them dry. Pierce each sweet potato several times with a fork.
3. Rub each sweet potato with olive oil and season with cumin, smoked paprika, garlic powder, salt, and black pepper.
4. Place the sweet potatoes on a baking sheet and bake for 40-45 minutes, or until they are tender and easily pierced with a fork.
5. Once baked, slice the sweet potatoes open lengthwise and fluff the insides with a fork.
6. Top each sweet potato with crumbled feta cheese, cherry tomatoes, kalamata olives, and fresh parsley.
7. For added creaminess, dollop Greek yogurt on top before serving, if desired.

Nutritional Information (per serving): 250 calories, 6g protein, 42g carbohydrates, 8g fat, 6g fiber, 15mg cholesterol, 340mg sodium, 710mg potassium.

BEEF AND EGGPLANT CASSEROLE

INGREDIENTS

- 1 small eggplant, sliced into rounds
- 1/2 lb lean ground beef
- 1/2 onion, diced; 2 cloves garlic, minced
- 1 can (14 oz) diced tomatoes, drained
- 1/2 tsp dried oregano; 1/2 tsp dried basil
- Salt and pepper to taste
- 1/2 cup shredded mozzarella cheese
- Fresh parsley for garnish

2

20 mins
40 mins

DIRECTIONS

1. Preheat your oven to 375°F (190°C).
2. Place the eggplant slices on a baking sheet lined with parchment paper. Lightly spray or brush them with olive oil and sprinkle with salt and pepper. Bake for about 15-20 minutes until tender.
3. In a skillet over medium heat, cook the ground beef, onion, and garlic until the meat is browned and the onions are softened.
4. Add the diced tomatoes, oregano, basil, salt, and pepper to the skillet. Stir well and let it simmer for 5-7 minutes.
5. Layer half of the cooked eggplant slices at the bottom in a small casserole dish. Top with half of the beef mixture and half of the shredded mozzarella. Repeat the layers.
6. Cover the casserole dish with foil and bake for 20 minutes. Then, remove the foil and bake for 5-10 minutes until the cheese is bubbly and golden. Garnish with fresh parsley before serving.

Nutritional Information (per serving): 468 calories, 34g protein, 24g carbohydrates, 28g fat, 7g fiber, 92mg cholesterol, 630mg sodium, 1241mg potassium.

BEEF KEBABS

INGREDIENTS

2
15 mins
10 mins

- 1/2 lb beef sirloin, cut into 1inch cubes
- 1/2 red bell pepper, cut into chunks
- 1/2 green bell pepper, cut into chunks
- 1/2 red onion, cut into chunks
- 8 cherry tomatoes; 2 tbsp olive oil
- 2 cloves garlic, minced
- 1 tsp dried oregano; 1/2 tsp dried thyme
- Salt and pepper to taste
- Lemon wedges for serving

DIRECTIONS

1. Mix the olive oil, minced garlic, dried oregano, dried thyme, salt, and pepper in a bowl. Add the beef cubes and coat them evenly with the marinade. Let it marinate for at least 10 minutes.
2. Preheat your grill or grill pan over medium-high heat.
3. Thread the marinated beef cubes onto skewers, alternating with the bell peppers, onion chunks, and cherry tomatoes.
4. Place the kebabs on the grill and cook for about 34 minutes per side until the beef is cooked to your desired doneness and the vegetables are charred and tender.
5. Remove the kebabs from the grill and let them rest for a few minutes before serving with lemon wedges on the side.

Nutritional Information (per serving): 422 calories, 31g protein, 11g carbohydrates, 29g fat, 3g fiber, 76mg cholesterol, 81mg sodium, 669mg potassium.

GREEK MOUSSAKA

INGREDIENTS

- 1 small eggplant, sliced into rounds
- 1/2 lb ground lamb or beef
- 1/2 onion, finely chopped; 2 cloves garlic, minced
- 1 can (14 oz) diced tomatoes, drained
- 1/2 tsp dried oregano
- Salt and pepper to taste
- 2 tbsp olive oil; 1 cup milk
- 2 tbsp all-purpose flour; 1/4 tsp ground nutmeg
- 1/2 cup grated Parmesan cheese; 1 egg, beaten
- Fresh parsley for garnish

2

30 mins

60 mins

DIRECTIONS

1. Preheat your oven to 375°F (190°C). Place the eggplant slices on a baking sheet, drizzle with olive oil, and sprinkle with salt and pepper. Bake for about 20 minutes until tender.
2. Heat 1 tablespoon of olive oil over medium heat in a skillet. Add the chopped onion and garlic, sautéing until softened. Add the ground lamb or beef, breaking it up with a spoon, and cook until browned.
3. Stir in the diced tomatoes, dried oregano, salt, and pepper. Let it simmer for 10-15 minutes.
4. Heat the remaining tablespoon of olive oil over medium heat in a separate saucepan. Whisk in the flour to make a roux, then gradually pour in the milk, whisking constantly until smooth and thickened. Stir in the ground nutmeg and half of the grated Parmesan cheese. Remove from heat and let it cool slightly.
5. Layer half of the cooked eggplant slices at the bottom in a greased baking dish. Spread the meat mixture over the eggplant layer. Top with the remaining eggplant slices.
6. Whisk the beaten egg into the milk and cheese mixture. Pour this sauce over the top of the moussaka, spreading it evenly.
7. Sprinkle the remaining grated Parmesan cheese on top. Bake for about 30-35 minutes until golden and bubbly.
8. Let the moussaka cool slightly before serving. Garnish with fresh parsley.

Nutritional Information (per serving): 726 calories, 37g protein, 28g carbohydrates, 51g fat, 8g fiber, 244mg cholesterol, 986mg sodium, 968mg potassium.

GYRO MEAT

INGREDIENTS

2

15 mins

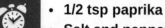

20 mins

- 1/2 lb ground lamb or beef
- 1/2 small onion, grated
- 2 cloves garlic, minced
- 1 tsp dried oregano
- 1/2 tsp dried thyme
- 1/2 tsp ground cumin
- 1/2 tsp paprika
- Salt and pepper to taste

DIRECTIONS

1. In a mixing bowl, mix the ground lamb or beef with grated onion, minced garlic, dried oregano, dried thyme, ground cumin, paprika, salt, and pepper. Mix well until all ingredients are evenly incorporated.
2. Shape the meat mixture into a loaf or log shape, about 1 inch thick.
3. Preheat a skillet over medium-high heat. Once hot, add the gyro meat and cook for about 8-10 minutes per side or until fully cooked and browned on the outside.
4. Remove the gyro meat from the skillet and let it rest briefly before slicing thinly.
5. Serve the gyro meat with pita bread, tzatziki sauce, sliced tomatoes, onions, and cucumbers.

Nutritional Information (per serving): 449 calories, 29g protein, 4g carbohydrates, 35g fat, 1g fiber, 116mg cholesterol, 181mg sodium, 307mg potassium.

BEEF STEW

INGREDIENTS

- 1/2 lb beef stew meat, cubed
- 1/2 onion, chopped
- 2 cloves garlic, minced
- 1 carrot, diced
- 1 celery stalk, diced
- 1 can (14 oz) diced tomatoes
- 1 cup beef broth
- 1/2 tsp dried oregano; 1/2 tsp dried basil
- Salt and pepper to taste; 1 tbsp olive oil
- Fresh parsley for garnish

2

15 mins

60 mins

DIRECTIONS

1. Heat the olive oil in a large pot or Dutch oven over medium heat. Add the chopped onion and minced garlic, sautéing until fragrant and translucent.

2. Add the beef stew meat to the pot and brown it on all sides, seasoning with salt and pepper.

3. Stir in the diced carrots and celery, cooking for a few minutes until slightly softened.

4. Add the diced tomatoes (including their juices), beef broth, dried oregano, and dried basil. Bring the stew to a boil, then reduce the heat to low and let it simmer, covered, for about 45 minutes to 1 hour, or until the beef is tender and the vegetables are cooked.

5. Adjust the seasoning with salt and pepper if needed. Serve the Mediterranean beef stew hot, garnished with fresh parsley.

Nutritional Information (per serving): 378 calories, 33g protein, 14g carbohydrates, 21g fat, 3g fiber, 80mg cholesterol, 875mg sodium, 798mg potassium.

LAMB KOFTA

INGREDIENTS

2

20 mins

15 mins

- 1/2 lb ground lamb
- 1/4 onion, finely chopped
- 2 cloves garlic, minced; 1/2 tsp ground cumin
- 1/2 tsp ground coriander; 1/2 tsp paprika
- 1/4 tsp ground cinnamon
- Salt and pepper to taste
- 1 tbsp chopped fresh parsley;
- 1 tbsp chopped fresh mint; 1 tbsp olive oil

DIRECTIONS

1. In a mixing bowl, combine the ground lamb, finely chopped onion, minced garlic, ground cumin, ground coriander, paprika, ground cinnamon, salt, pepper, chopped parsley, and chopped mint. Mix well until all ingredients are evenly distributed.

2. Divide the lamb mixture into four equal portions and shape each portion into a cylindrical kofta shape.

3. Preheat a grill or grill pan over medium-high heat. Brush the koftas with olive oil.

4. Grill the koftas for 5-7 minutes per side or until cooked through and nicely browned on the outside.

5. Remove the koftas from the grill and let them rest for a few minutes before serving.

Nutritional Information (per serving): 415 calories, 23g protein, 2g carbohydrates, 35g fat, 1g fiber, 87mg cholesterol, 100mg sodium, 174mg potassium.

LAMB STEW

INGREDIENTS

- 1/2 lb lamb stew meat, cubed
- 1/2 onion, chopped
- 2 cloves garlic, minced
- 1 carrot, diced; 1 celery stalk, diced
- 1 can (14 oz) diced tomatoes
- 1 cup beef broth
- 1/2 tsp dried oregano; 1/2 tsp dried thyme
- Salt and pepper to taste; 1 tbsp olive oil
- Fresh parsley for garnish

2

15 mins

60 mins

DIRECTIONS

1. Heat olive oil over medium heat in a large pot or Dutch oven. Add chopped onion and minced garlic, sautéing until softened and fragrant.
2. Add cubed lamb stew meat to the pot, season with salt and pepper, and cook until browned on all sides.
3. Stir in diced carrots, celery, tomatoes (including juices), beef broth, dried oregano, and dried thyme. Bring to a boil.
4. Reduce heat to low, cover, and let the stew simmer for about 45 minutes to 1 hour, or until the lamb is tender and the vegetables are cooked.
5. Adjust seasoning with salt and pepper if needed. Serve the Mediterranean lamb stew hot, garnished with fresh parsley.

Nutritional Information (per serving): 480 calories, 38g protein, 12g carbohydrates, 32g fat, 3g fiber, 90mg cholesterol, 760mg sodium, 740mg potassium.

LAMB BURGERS

INGREDIENTS

2

15 mins

10 mins

- 1/2 lb ground lamb
- 1/4 onion, finely chopped
- 2 cloves garlic, minced
- 1/2 tsp dried oregano
- 1/2 tsp dried mint; 1/4 tsp ground cumin
- Salt and pepper to taste; 2 hamburger buns
- Lettuce, tomato, and red onion slices for serving
- Tzatziki sauce for topping (optional)

DIRECTIONS

1. Combine ground lamb, finely chopped onion, minced garlic, dried oregano, mint, ground cumin, salt, and pepper in a mixing bowl. Mix until well combined.
2. Divide the lamb mixture into two portions and shape each into a burger patty.
3. Preheat a grill or grill pan over medium-high heat. Cook the lamb burgers for about 4-5 minutes per side or until they reach your desired level of doneness.
4. Toast the hamburger buns on the grill for a minute or until lightly golden.
5. Assemble the lamb burgers by placing lettuce, tomato, and red onion slices on the bottom bun, followed by the cooked lamb patty. If desired, top with tzatziki sauce and cover with the top bun.

Nutritional Information (per serving): 492 calories, 25g protein, 27g carbohydrates, 31g fat, 2g fiber, 80mg cholesterol, 568mg sodium, 310mg potassium.

CHICKEN SKILLET

INGREDIENTS

- 2 boneless, skinless chicken breasts cut into cubes
- 1/2 onion, chopped; 2 cloves garlic, minced
- 1/2 red bell pepper, chopped;
- 1/2 yellow bell pepper, chopped
- 1 can (14 oz) diced tomatoes, drained
- 1/2 tsp dried oregano; 1/2 tsp dried basil
- Salt and pepper to taste; 1 tbsp olive oil
- 1/4 cup crumbled feta cheese;
- Fresh parsley for garnish

2

10 mins

20 mins

DIRECTIONS

1. Heat olive oil in a skillet over medium-high heat. Add chopped onion and minced garlic, sautéing until softened and fragrant.
2. Add cubed chicken breasts to the skillet and cook until browned on all sides.
3. Stir in chopped red and yellow bell peppers, cooking for a few minutes until slightly softened.
4. Add diced tomatoes (drained), dried oregano, dried basil, salt, and pepper. Stir well to combine.
5. Reduce heat to low, cover the skillet, and let it simmer for 10 minutes until the chicken is cooked and the flavors meld together.
6. Sprinkle crumbled feta cheese over the chicken mixture and let it melt slightly.
7. Garnish with fresh parsley before serving.

Nutritional Information (per serving): 372 calories, 38g protein, 14g carbohydrates, 18g fat, 3g fiber, 92mg cholesterol, 712mg sodium, 676mg potassium.

CHICKEN SKILLET WITH MUSHROOMS AND SLIVERED PARMESAN

INGREDIENTS

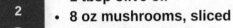

2

10 mins
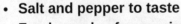
20 mins

- 2 boneless, skinless chicken breasts, sliced
- 1 tbsp olive oil
- 8 oz mushrooms, sliced
- 2 cloves garlic, minced
- 1/4 cup slivered Parmesan cheese
- 1/2 tsp dried thyme
- Salt and pepper to taste
- Fresh parsley for garnish

DIRECTIONS

1. Heat olive oil in a skillet over medium heat. Add sliced chicken breasts and cook until browned on both sides and cooked through. Remove chicken from skillet and set aside.
2. In the same skillet, add sliced mushrooms and minced garlic. Sauté until mushrooms are tender and golden brown.
3. Return the cooked chicken to the skillet. Sprinkle dried thyme, salt, and pepper over the chicken-mushroom mixture. Stir well to combine and let it cook for a few more minutes.
4. Sprinkle slivered Parmesan cheese evenly over the chicken and mushrooms. Cover the skillet and cook for 2-3 minutes or until the cheese melts.
5. Garnish with fresh parsley before serving.

Nutritional Information (per serving): 315 calories, 38g protein, 5g carbohydrates, 15g fat, 1g fiber, 97mg cholesterol, 372mg sodium, 690mg potassium.

DUTCH OVEN CHICKEN THIGHS

INGREDIENTS

- 4 chicken thighs, bonein and skinon
- 1 tbsp olive oil
- 1/2 onion, chopped
- 2 cloves garlic, minced
- 1/2 cup cherry tomatoes, halved
- 1/4 cup Kalamata olives, pitted
- 1/4 cup sundried tomatoes, chopped
- 1/2 tsp dried oregano
- Salt and pepper to taste
- Fresh parsley for garnish

2

15 mins

45 mins

DIRECTIONS

1. Preheat your oven to 375°F (190°C).

2. Heat olive oil in a Dutch oven over medium heat. Add chopped onion and minced garlic, sautéing until softened and fragrant.

3. Season the chicken thighs with salt, pepper, and dried oregano. Add them to the Dutch oven, skin side down, and sear until golden brown, about 5 minutes per side.

4. In the Dutch oven, scatter halved cherry tomatoes, pitted Kalamata olives, and chopped sundried tomatoes around the chicken.

5. Cover the Dutch oven with a lid and transfer it to the preheated oven. Bake for 30-35 minutes or until the chicken is cooked through and tender.

6. Garnish with fresh parsley before serving.

Nutritional Information (per serving): 482 calories, 35g protein, 10g carbohydrates, 35g fat, 3g fiber, 143mg cholesterol, 543mg sodium, 624mg potassium.

MOROCCAN CHICKEN TAGINE

INGREDIENTS

2

15 mins

40 mins

- 2 chicken thighs, bone-in and skin-on; 1 tbsp olive oil
- 1/2 onion, chopped; 2 cloves garlic, minced
- 1/2 tsp ground cumin; 1/2 tsp ground coriander
- 1/2 tsp paprika; 1/4 tsp ground cinnamon
- Salt and pepper to taste
- 1/2 cup chicken broth
- 1/4 cup dried apricots, chopped
- 1/4 cup green olives, pitted
- Fresh cilantro for garnish

DIRECTIONS

1. Heat olive oil in a tagine or large skillet over medium heat. Add chopped onion and minced garlic, sautéing until softened and fragrant.

2. Season chicken thighs with ground cumin, coriander, paprika, cinnamon, salt, and pepper. Add them to the tagine or skillet, skin side down, and sear until golden brown, about 5 minutes per side.

3. Pour chicken broth into the tagine or skillet. Add chopped dried apricots and pitted green olives.

4. Cover the tagine or skillet with a lid and let it simmer for 30 minutes or until the chicken is cooked through and tender and the sauce has thickened.

5. Garnish with fresh cilantro before serving.

Nutritional Information (per serving): 475 calories, 24g protein, 12g carbohydrates, 35g fat, 2g fiber, 92mg cholesterol, 682mg sodium, 471mg potassium.

GREEK TURKEY MEATBALLS

INGREDIENTS

- 1 lb ground turkey
- 1/4 cup breadcrumbs (preferably whole wheat)
- 1/4 cup feta cheese, crumbled
- 1/4 cup fresh parsley, chopped
- 1 clove garlic, minced; 1 tsp dried oregano
- 1/2 tsp salt; 1/4 tsp black pepper
- 1 egg, lightly beaten; 2 tbsp olive oil
- 1/2 cup marinara sauce (for serving)
- Lemon wedges (for garnish)

2

15 mins

25 mins

DIRECTIONS

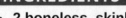

1. Preheat the oven to 400°F (200°C).

2. In a large mixing bowl, combine the ground turkey, breadcrumbs, feta cheese, parsley, minced garlic, oregano, salt, black pepper, and beaten egg. Mix until well combined.

3. Form the mixture into meatballs, about 1 inch in diameter, and place them on a baking sheet lined with parchment paper.

4. Drizzle olive oil over the meatballs and bake in the preheated oven for 20-25 minutes, or until cooked through and golden brown.

5. While the meatballs are baking, heat the marinara sauce in a small saucepan over low heat.

6. Serve the meatballs warm with marinara sauce on the side, garnished with lemon wedges.

Nutritional Information (per serving): 335 calories, 30g protein, 14g carbohydrates, 18g fat, 1g fiber, 93mg cholesterol, 582mg sodium, 445mg potassium.

GREEK LEMON CHICKEN

INGREDIENTS

2

10 mins

20 mins

- 2 boneless, skinless chicken breasts
- Salt and pepper to taste
- 2 tbsp olive oil
- 2 cloves garlic, minced
- 1 lemon, zest and juice
- 1/2 tsp dried oregano
- 1/4 cup chicken broth
- Fresh parsley for garnish

DIRECTIONS

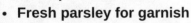

1. Season chicken breasts with salt and pepper on both sides.

2. Heat olive oil in a skillet over medium-high heat. Add minced garlic and sauté until fragrant.

3. Add chicken breasts to the skillet, cook until golden brown on both sides, and cook through for about 5-7 minutes per side.

4. In a small bowl, combine lemon zest, juice, dried oregano, and chicken broth. Pour the mixture over the chicken in the skillet.

5. Let the chicken simmer in the lemon sauce for a few minutes until the sauce thickens slightly and coats the chicken. Garnish with fresh parsley before serving.

Nutritional Information (per serving): 302 calories, 32g protein, 3g carbohydrates, 18g fat, 1g fiber, 87mg cholesterol, 405mg sodium, 366mg potassium.

ITALIAN HERB BAKED CHICKEN THIGHS

INGREDIENTS

2

10 mins

25 mins

- 4 bonein, skinon chicken thighs
- 2 tbsp olive oil
- 2 cloves garlic, minced
- 1 tsp dried Italian herbs (such as oregano, basil, thyme)
- Salt and pepper to taste
- Fresh parsley for garnish

DIRECTIONS

1. Preheat your oven to 400°F (200°C).
2. Add olive oil, minced garlic, dried Italian herbs, salt, and pepper in a small bowl.
3. Pat the chicken thighs dry with paper towels and place them in a baking dish.
4. Brush the olive oil and herb mixture over the chicken thighs, coating them evenly.
5. Bake the chicken thighs in the preheated oven for about 20-25 minutes or until they reach an internal temperature of 165°F (74°C) and the skin is crispy and golden brown.
6. Garnish with fresh parsley before serving.

Nutritional Information (per serving): 392 calories, 32g protein, 1g carbohydrates, 29g fat, 0g fiber, 140mg cholesterol, 254mg sodium, 312mg potassium.

CHICKEN STEW

INGREDIENTS

2

15 mins

30 mins

- 2 boneless, skinless chicken breasts, cubed
- 1 tbsp olive oil; 1/2 onion, chopped
- 2 cloves garlic, minced
- 1 carrot, sliced; 1 celery stalk, sliced
- 1/2 cup diced tomatoes; 1 cup chicken broth
- 1/2 tsp dried thyme
- Salt and pepper to taste
- Fresh parsley for garnish

DIRECTIONS

1. Heat olive oil in a pot over medium heat. Add chopped onion and minced garlic, sautéing until softened and fragrant.
2. Add cubed chicken breasts to the pot and cook until lightly browned on all sides.
3. Stir in sliced carrot and celery, diced tomatoes, chicken broth, dried thyme, salt, and pepper. Bring the mixture to a simmer.
4. Reduce heat to low, cover the pot, and let the stew simmer for about 20-25 minutes or until the chicken is cooked and the vegetables are tender.
5. Adjust seasoning with salt and pepper if needed. Garnish with fresh parsley before serving.

Nutritional Information (per serving): 288 calories, 32g protein, 11g carbohydrates, 13g fat, 2g fiber, 76mg cholesterol, 788mg sodium, 520mg potassium.

• FISH AND SEAFOOD •

BAKED WHOLE FISH

INGREDIENTS

- 1 whole fish (such as sea bass or snapper), cleaned and gutted
- 2 tbsp olive oil
- 2 cloves garlic, minced
- 1 lemon, sliced
- Salt and pepper to taste
- Fresh herbs (such as parsley or dill) for garnish

2

15 mins

25 mins

DIRECTIONS

1. Preheat your oven to 400°F (200°C) and line a baking dish with parchment paper.
2. Rinse the whole fish under cold water and pat it dry with paper towels. Score the fish on both sides with diagonal cuts.
3. Rub the fish with olive oil, minced garlic, salt, and pepper, and coat it evenly.
4. Stuff the cavity of the fish with lemon slices and any additional herbs you like.
5. Place the fish in the prepared baking dish and bake in the oven for 20-25 minutes or until it flakes easily with a fork.
6. Remove the fish from the oven and let it rest for a few minutes before serving. Garnish with fresh herbs.

Nutritional Information (per serving): 240 calories, 35g protein, 0g carbohydrates, 11g fat, 0g fiber, 85mg cholesterol, 98mg sodium, 440mg potassium.

GRILLED SALMON
WITH LEMON AND HERBS

INGREDIENTS

2

10 mins

10 mins

- 2 salmon fillets (6 oz each)
- 2 tbsp olive oil
- 1 lemon, sliced
- 2 cloves garlic, minced
- 1 tsp dried dill
- Salt and pepper to taste
- Fresh parsley for garnish

DIRECTIONS

1. Preheat your grill to medium-high heat.
2. In a small bowl, add olive oil, minced garlic, dried dill, salt, and pepper.
3. Rub the salmon fillets with the olive oil and herb mixture, ensuring they are coated evenly.
4. Place lemon slices on top of each salmon fillet.
5. Grill the salmon for about 4-5 minutes per side or until it flakes easily with a fork and is cooked to your desired doneness.
6. Remove the grilled salmon from the heat and garnish with fresh parsley before serving.

Nutritional Information (per serving): 358 calories, 34g protein, 5g carbohydrates, 22g fat, 1g fiber, 85mg cholesterol, 238mg sodium, 620mg potassium.

GREEK STYLE BAKED FISH

INGREDIENTS

- 2 fish fillets (such as cod or tilapia), about 6 oz each
- 2 tbsp olive oil
- 2 cloves garlic, minced
- 1 tsp dried oregano
- 1 tsp dried thyme
- 1/2 tsp paprika
- Salt and pepper to taste
- Lemon wedges for serving
- Fresh parsley for garnish

2

10 mins

20 mins

DIRECTIONS

1. Preheat your oven to 400°F (200°C). Line a baking dish with parchment paper.
2. Pat the fish fillets dry with paper towels and place them in the prepared baking dish.
3. Add olive oil, minced garlic, dried oregano, dried thyme, paprika, salt, and pepper in a small bowl.
4. Brush the olive oil and herb mixture evenly over the fish fillets, coating them well.
5. Bake the fish in the preheated oven for 15-20 minutes or until it flakes easily with a fork and is cooked through.
6. Remove the baked fish from the oven and garnish with fresh parsley. Serve with lemon wedges on the side.

Nutritional Information (per serving): 320 calories, 28g protein, 3g carbohydrates, 21g fat, 1g fiber, 65mg cholesterol, 302mg sodium, 420mg potassium.

MEDITERRANEAN SHRIMP PASTA

INGREDIENTS

2

15 mins

15 mins

- 6 oz spaghetti or linguine pasta
- 8 oz shrimp, peeled and deveined
- 2 tbsp olive oil
- 2 cloves garlic, minced
- 1/2 cup cherry tomatoes, halved
- 1/4 cup Kalamata olives, pitted and sliced
- 1/4 cup chopped fresh parsley
- 1/4 tsp red pepper flakes (optional)
- Salt and pepper to taste
- Grated Parmesan cheese for serving (optional)

DIRECTIONS

1. Cook the pasta according to the package instructions until al dente. Drain and set aside.
2. In a large skillet, heat olive oil over medium heat. Add minced garlic and sauté until fragrant.
3. Add shrimp to the skillet and cook until pink and opaque, about 2-3 minutes per side.
4. Stir in halved cherry tomatoes, sliced Kalamata olives, chopped fresh parsley, and red pepper flakes (if using). Cook for another 2 minutes to heat through.
5. Add the cooked pasta to the skillet with the shrimp and vegetables. Toss everything together until well combined.
6. Season with salt and pepper to taste. If desired, serve the Mediterranean shrimp pasta hot, topped with grated Parmesan cheese.

Nutritional Information (per serving): 485 calories, 35g protein, 52g carbohydrates, 15g fat, 4g fiber, 174mg cholesterol, 382mg sodium, 438mg potassium.

SEAFOOD PAELLA

INGREDIENTS

- 2 fish fillets (such as cod or tilapia), about 6 oz each
- 2 tbsp olive oil
- 2 cloves garlic, minced
- 1 tsp dried oregano
- 1 tsp dried thyme
- 1/2 tsp paprika
- Salt and pepper to taste
- Lemon wedges for serving
- Fresh parsley for garnish

2

15 mins

30 mins

DIRECTIONS

1. Heat olive oil in a large skillet or paella pan over medium heat. Add chopped onion, minced garlic, and diced red bell pepper. Sauté until vegetables are softened.
2. Stir in diced tomato, smoked paprika, and saffron threads. Cook for another minute.
3. Add Arborio rice to the skillet and stir to coat the rice with the vegetable mixture.
4. Pour chicken or seafood broth into the skillet. Bring to a simmer and cook for about 15 minutes or until the rice is almost tender.
5. Arrange shrimp, mussels, and squid rings over the rice in the skillet. Cover and cook for another 10 minutes or until the seafood is cooked and the mussels have opened.
6. Season with salt and pepper to taste. Garnish with fresh parsley and serve with lemon wedges.

Nutritional Information (per serving): 552 calories, 43g protein, 60g carbohydrates, 16g fat, 4g fiber, 176mg cholesterol, 864mg sodium, 678mg potassium.

BAKED STUFFED SQUID

INGREDIENTS

- 4 small squid tubes, cleaned and tentacles reserved
- 1/2 cup cooked rice
- 1/4 cup chopped tomatoes; 1/4 cup chopped onion
- 2 cloves garlic, minced
- 2 tbsp olive oil
- 1 tbsp chopped fresh parsley
- 1/2 tsp dried oregano; Salt and pepper to taste
- Lemon wedges for serving
- Fresh parsley for garnish

2

20 mins

25 mins

DIRECTIONS

1. Preheat your oven to 375°F (190°C).
2. In a bowl, combine cooked rice, chopped tomatoes, chopped onion, minced garlic, olive oil, chopped parsley, dried oregano, salt, and pepper. Mix well to make the stuffing.
3. Stuff the cleaned squid tubes with the prepared stuffing mixture, leaving some space at the top to allow for expansion during baking. Secure the ends of the squid tubes with toothpicks.
4. Place the stuffed squid tubes and reserved tentacles in a baking dish. Drizzle with olive oil and season with salt and pepper.
5. Bake in the preheated oven for about 20-25 minutes or until the squid is cooked through and tender.
6. Remove the toothpicks from the squid tubes before serving. Garnish with fresh parsley and serve with lemon wedges on the side.

Nutritional Information (per serving): 346 calories, 27g protein, 22g carbohydrates, 16g fat, 1g fiber, 250mg cholesterol, 584mg sodium, 520mg potassium.

MUSSELS MARINARA

INGREDIENTS

- 1 lb fresh mussels, cleaned and debearded
- 2 tbsp olive oil
- 2 cloves garlic, minced
- 1/2 onion, chopped
- 1/2 cup marinara sauce
- 1/4 cup white wine
- 1 tbsp chopped fresh parsley
- Salt and pepper to taste
- Crushed red pepper flakes (optional)
- Crusty bread for serving

2

10 mins

15 mins

DIRECTIONS

1. Heat olive oil in a large pot over medium heat. Add minced garlic and chopped onion, sautéing until softened and fragrant.

2. Add marinara sauce and white wine to the pot. Stir well to combine.

3. Add the cleaned mussels to the pot and cover with a lid. Cook for about 5-7 minutes or until the mussels have opened, shaking the pot occasionally.

4. Discard any unopened mussels. If using, season the mussels marinara with salt, pepper, and crushed red pepper flakes. Stir in chopped fresh parsley.

5. Serve the mussels marinara hot, with crusty bread on the side, for dipping into the flavorful sauce.

Nutritional Information (per serving): 303 calories, 24g protein, 12g carbohydrates, 16g fat, 1g fiber, 47mg cholesterol, 832mg sodium, 464mg potassium.

TILAPIA TACOS

INGREDIENTS

2

15 mins

10 mins

- 2 tilapia fillets (about 6 oz each)
- 1 tbsp olive oil; 1 tsp chili powder
- 1/2 tsp ground cumin; 1/2 tsp garlic powder
- Salt and pepper to taste
- 4 small whole wheat or corn tortillas
- 1/2 cup shredded cabbage or lettuce
- 1/4 cup diced tomatoes
- 1/4 cup diced red onion
- Fresh cilantro leaves for garnish
- Lime wedges for serving

DIRECTIONS

1. In a small bowl, mix chili powder, ground cumin, garlic powder, salt, and pepper.
2. Rub the tilapia fillets with olive oil and sprinkle the spice mixture evenly on both sides of the fillets.
3. Heat a nonstick skillet over medium-high heat. Add the seasoned tilapia fillets to the skillet and cook for 3-4 minutes per side or until cooked through and easily flaked with a fork.
4. Warm the tortillas in the skillet for about 30 seconds on each side or until softened and heated through.
5. To assemble the tacos, place a portion of shredded cabbage or lettuce on each tortilla, followed by a cooked tilapia fillet—top with diced tomatoes, red onion, and fresh cilantro leaves. Serve with lime wedges on the side.

Nutritional Information (per serving): 292 calories, 31g protein, 21g carbohydrates, 10g fat, 4g fiber, 70mg cholesterol, 422mg sodium, 574mg potassium.

LINGUINE WITH CREAMY WHITE CLAM SAUCE

INGREDIENTS

- 6 oz linguine pasta
- 1 tbsp olive oil
- 2 cloves garlic, minced
- 1/2 cup clam juice
- 1/4 cup white wine
- 1/2 cup heavy cream
- 1/2 cup grated Parmesan cheese
- 1 can (5 oz) chopped clams, drained
- Salt and pepper to taste
- Fresh parsley for garnish

2

10 mins

15 mins

DIRECTIONS

1. Cook the linguine pasta according to the package instructions until al dente. Drain and set aside.
2. Heat olive oil over medium heat in a large skillet. Add minced garlic and sauté until fragrant.
3. Add the clam juice and white wine. Bring to a simmer and cook for about 2 minutes.
4. Stir in heavy cream and grated Parmesan cheese. Cook for another 3-4 minutes until the sauce thickens slightly.
5. Add the drained, chopped clams to the skillet and heat through.
6. Season the creamy white clam sauce with salt and pepper to taste. Toss the cooked linguine pasta in the sauce until well coated.
7. Serve the linguine hot with creamy white clam sauce, garnished with fresh parsley.

Nutritional Information (per serving): 643 calories, 25g protein, 56g carbohydrates, 34g fat, 2g fiber, 103mg cholesterol, 560mg sodium, 302mg potassium.

COD WITH ROASTED TOMATOES

INGREDIENTS

2

10 mins

20 mins

- 2 cod fillets (about 6 oz each)
- 1 cup cherry tomatoes, halved
- 2 tbsp olive oil
- 2 cloves garlic, minced
- 1 tsp dried oregano
- Salt and pepper to taste
- Lemon wedges for serving
- Fresh parsley for garnish

DIRECTIONS

1. Preheat your oven to 400°F (200°C). Line a baking sheet with parchment paper.
2. Place the halved cherry tomatoes on the prepared baking sheet. Drizzle with one tablespoon of olive oil and season with minced garlic, dried oregano, salt, and pepper. Toss to coat evenly.
3. Roast the tomatoes in the oven for 10-12 minutes or until they soften and caramelize.
4. Meanwhile, pat the cod fillets dry with paper towels—season both sides of the fillets with salt and pepper.
5. Heat the remaining tablespoon of olive oil in a skillet over medium-high heat. Add the cod fillets and cook for about 3-4 minutes per side or until golden brown and cooked through.
6. Serve the cooked cod fillets with the roasted tomatoes on top. Garnish with fresh parsley and serve with lemon wedges on the side.

Nutritional Information (per serving): 325 calories, 35g protein, 8g carbohydrates, 17g fat, 2g fiber, 75mg cholesterol, 310mg sodium, 680mg potassium.

• BEANS AND GRAINS •

MEDITERRANEAN COUSCOUS PILAF

INGREDIENTS

- 1/2 cup couscous
- 1 cup vegetable broth
- 1 tbsp olive oil; 1/4 cup chopped onion
- 1/4 cup chopped bell pepper (any color)
- 1/4 cup chopped zucchini; 1/4 cup chopped tomatoes
- 2 tbsp chopped fresh parsley; 1/4 tsp dried oregano
- Salt and pepper to taste; Lemon wedges for serving

2

10 mins

15 mins

DIRECTIONS

1. In a saucepan, bring the vegetable broth to a boil. Stir in the couscous, cover with a lid, and remove from heat. Let it sit for about 5 minutes or until the couscous has absorbed the broth and is tender.

2. Heat olive oil over medium heat in a skillet. Add chopped onion, bell pepper, and zucchini. Sauté until the vegetables are softened.

3. Stir in chopped tomatoes, parsley, dried oregano, salt, and pepper. Cook for another 2-3 minutes to combine the flavors.

4. Fluff the cooked couscous with a fork and transfer it to the skillet with the vegetables. Stir well to mix everything.

5. Cook the couscous pilaf for a few more minutes until heated through.

6. Serve the Mediterranean couscous pilaf hot, garnished with fresh parsley and lemon wedges on the side.

Nutritional Information (per serving): 240 calories, 6g protein, 39g carbohydrates, 7g fat, 4g fiber, 0mg cholesterol, 460mg sodium, 290mg potassium.

BUTTER BEANS WITH GARLIC, LEMON, AND HERBS

INGREDIENTS

2

10 mins

15 mins

- 1 can (15 oz) butter beans, drained and rinsed
- 2 tbsp olive oil
- 2 cloves garlic, minced
- Zest of 1 lemon
- 1 tbsp lemon juice
- 1 tsp dried thyme
- Salt and pepper to taste
- Fresh parsley for garnish (optional)

DIRECTIONS

1. Heat olive oil in a skillet over medium heat. Add minced garlic and sauté until fragrant, about 1 minute.

2. Add the drained and rinsed butter beans to the skillet. Stir to combine with the garlic.

3. Add lemon zest, juice, dried thyme, salt, and pepper to the beans. Mix well.

4. Cook the beans for about 10-12 minutes, stirring occasionally, until heated through and infused with the flavors.

5. Remove the skillet from heat. Garnish with fresh parsley if desired.

6. Serve the butter beans with garlic, lemon, and herbs as a side dish or as part of a Mediterranean inspired meal.

Nutritional Information (per serving): 286 calories, 9g protein, 30g carbohydrates, 15g fat, 6g fiber, 0mg cholesterol, 589mg sodium, 498mg potassium.

SPANISH RICE AND BEANS

2

10 mins

25 mins

INGREDIENTS

- 1/2 cup long-grain white rice
- 1 cup water or vegetable broth
- 1 tbsp olive oil
- 1/2 onion, chopped; 1/2 bell pepper, chopped
- 1 clove garlic, minced
- 1 can (15 oz) black beans, drained and rinsed
- 1/2 tsp ground cumin
- 1/2 tsp smoked paprika
- Salt and pepper to taste
- Fresh cilantro for garnish (optional)

DIRECTIONS

1. Rinse the rice under cold water until the water runs clear. Drain well.

2. Heat olive oil over medium heat in a saucepan. Add chopped onion, bell pepper, and minced garlic. Sauté until softened, about 5 minutes.

3. Add the rinsed rice to the saucepan and stir to coat with the vegetables and oil.

4. Pour in the water or vegetable broth and boil. Reduce heat to low, cover, and simmer for 15-18 minutes or until the rice is cooked and liquid is absorbed.

5. Stir in the drained and rinsed black beans, ground cumin, smoked paprika, salt, and pepper. Cook for 5-7 minutes until heated through and flavors are combined.

6. Remove from heat and let it sit, covered, for a few minutes before serving. Garnish with fresh cilantro if desired.

Nutritional Information (per serving): 315 calories, 11g protein, 56g carbohydrates, 6g fat, 9g fiber, 0mg cholesterol, 460mg sodium, 505mg potassium.

GRAIN BOWLS WITH LENTILS AND CHICKPEAS

INGREDIENTS

2

15 mins

20 mins

- 1/2 cup brown rice; 1/2 cup green lentils
- 1 can (15 oz) chickpeas, drained and rinsed
- 1 cup cherry tomatoes, halved
- 1/2 cucumber, diced
- 1/4 red onion, thinly sliced
- 2 tbsp chopped fresh parsley
- 2 tbsp chopped fresh mint
- 1/4 cup crumbled feta cheese
- 2 tbsp olive oil; 1 tbsp lemon juice
- Salt and pepper to taste

DIRECTIONS

1. According to package instructions, Cook the brown rice and green lentils separately. Once cooked, let them cool slightly.

2. In a large bowl, combine the cooked brown rice, lentils, chickpeas, cherry tomatoes, cucumber, red onion, chopped parsley, chopped mint, and crumbled feta cheese.

3. Whisk the olive oil, lemon juice, salt, and pepper in a small bowl to make the dressing.

4. Pour the dressing over the grain and vegetable mixture. Toss gently to coat everything evenly with the dressing.

5. Divide the mixture into two serving bowls.

6. Serve the Mediterranean grain bowls with lentils and chickpeas immediately or refrigerate until ready to eat.

Nutritional Information (per serving): 535 calories, 22g protein, 82g carbohydrates, 15g fat, 19g fiber, 0mg cholesterol, 536mg sodium, 1021mg potassium.

ROASTED WHITE BEANS WITH VEGETABLES GREEK STYLE

INGREDIENTS

2

10 mins

25 mins

- 1 can (15 oz) white beans, drained and rinsed
- 1 cup cherry tomatoes, halved
- 1/2 red bell pepper, diced;
- 1/2 yellow bell pepper, diced
- 1/2 red onion, sliced; 2 cloves garlic, minced
- 2 tbsp olive oil; 1 tsp dried oregano
- 1/2 tsp dried thyme; Salt and pepper to taste
- Fresh parsley for garnish (optional)
- Crumbled feta cheese for serving (optional)

DIRECTIONS

1. Preheat the oven to 400°F (200°C) and line a baking sheet with parchment paper.
2. In a large bowl, combine the drained and rinsed white beans, halved cherry tomatoes, diced bell peppers, sliced red onion, minced garlic, olive oil, dried oregano, dried thyme, salt, and pepper. Toss to coat everything evenly.
3. Spread the bean and vegetable mixture in a single layer on the prepared baking sheet.
4. Roast in the oven for about 20-25 minutes or until the vegetables are tender and slightly caramelized.
5. Remove from the oven and let it cool slightly. Garnish with fresh parsley and crumbled feta cheese if desired.
6. For a complete meal, Serve the roasted white beans with Greek vegetables as a side dish or overcooked grains like quinoa or couscous.

Nutritional Information (per serving): 320 calories, 12g protein, 40g carbohydrates, 14g fat, 8g fiber, 0mg cholesterol, 420mg sodium, 780mg potassium.

MEDITERRANEAN GRAIN BOWLS

INGREDIENTS

2

15 mins

20 mins

- 1/2 cup quinoa; 1/2 cup bulgur wheat
- 1 cup water or vegetable broth
- 1/2 cucumber, diced; 1/2 cup cherry tomatoes, halved
- 1/4 cup Kalamata olives, pitted and sliced
- 1/4 cup crumbled feta cheese
- 2 tbsp chopped fresh parsley;
- 2 tbsp chopped fresh mint
- 2 tbsp olive oil
- 1 tbsp lemon juice; Salt and pepper to taste

DIRECTIONS

1. Rinse the quinoa and bulgur wheat under cold water. Combine the quinoa, bulgur wheat, and water or vegetable broth in a saucepan. Bring to a boil, then reduce heat, cover, and simmer for 15 minutes or until the liquid is absorbed and the grains are tender.
2. In a large bowl, combine the cooked quinoa and bulgur wheat with diced cucumber, cherry tomatoes, sliced Kalamata olives, crumbled feta cheese, chopped parsley, and chopped mint.
3. To make the dressing, whisk together olive oil, lemon juice, salt, and pepper in a small bowl.
4. Pour the dressing over the grain and vegetable mixture. Toss gently to coat everything evenly with the dressing. Divide the mixture into two serving bowls.
6. Serve the Mediterranean grain bowls immediately or refrigerate until ready to eat.

Nutritional Information (per serving): 440 calories, 13g protein, 55g carbohydrates, 19g fat, 9g fiber, 11mg cholesterol, 730mg sodium, 670mg potassium.

CHICKPEA STEW

INGREDIENTS

- 1 can (15 oz) chickpeas, drained and rinsed
- 1 onion, chopped
- 2 cloves garlic, minced
- 1 carrot, diced; 1 celery stalk, diced
- 1 red bell pepper, diced
- 1 can (15 oz) diced tomatoes
- 1 cup vegetable broth
- 1 tsp dried thyme; 1 tsp paprika
- Salt and pepper to taste; 2 tbsp olive oil
- Fresh parsley for garnish (optional)

2

10 mins

25 mins

DIRECTIONS

1. Heat olive oil over medium heat in a large pot. Add chopped onion and garlic, and sauté until translucent.
2. Add diced carrot, celery, and red bell pepper to the pot. Cook for about 5 minutes until vegetables are slightly softened.
3. Stir in drained and rinsed chickpeas, diced tomatoes (with juices), vegetable broth, dried thyme, paprika, salt, and pepper. Bring to a simmer.
4. Reduce the heat to low, cover the pot, and let the stew simmer for 15-20 minutes to allow the flavors to blend and the vegetables to become tender.
5. Adjust seasoning if needed. Serve the chickpea stew hot, garnished with fresh parsley if desired.

Nutritional Information (per serving): 320 calories, 12g protein, 45g carbohydrates, 10g fat, 10g fiber, 0mg cholesterol, 780mg sodium, 680mg potassium.

HUMMUS

INGREDIENTS

2

10 mins

0 mins

- 1 can (15 oz) chickpeas, drained and rinsed
- 2 tbsp tahini
- 2 tbsp olive oil
- 2 cloves garlic, minced
- 2 tbsp lemon juice
- Salt to taste
- Water (as needed for desired consistency)
- Optional toppings: paprika, chopped parsley, a drizzle of olive oil

DIRECTIONS

1. In a food processor, combine chickpeas, tahini, olive oil, minced garlic, lemon juice, and a pinch of salt.
2. Blend the ingredients until smooth, scraping down the sides of the processor as needed.
3. If the hummus is too thick, gradually add water, one tablespoon at a time, until you reach your desired consistency.
4. Taste and adjust seasoning, adding more salt or lemon juice if needed.
5. Transfer the hummus to a serving bowl. Drizzle with olive oil and sprinkle with paprika and chopped parsley, if desired.
6. Serve the hummus with pita bread, crackers, or vegetables for dipping.

Nutritional Information (per serving): 260 calories, 9g protein, 21g carbohydrates, 16g fat, 6g fiber, 0mg cholesterol, 310mg sodium, 310mg potassium.

FALAFEL

INGREDIENTS

- 1 can (15 oz) chickpeas, drained and rinsed
- 1/2 small onion, chopped
- 2 cloves garlic, minced
- 2 tbsp chopped fresh parsley
- 1 tbsp chopped fresh cilantro
- 1 tsp ground cumin; 1/2 tsp ground coriander
- 1/4 tsp cayenne pepper (optional)
- Salt to taste
- 2 tbsp all-purpose flour; 1/2 tsp baking powder
- Vegetable oil for frying

2
15 mins
15 mins

DIRECTIONS

1. In a food processor, combine chickpeas, onion, garlic, parsley, cilantro, cumin, coriander, cayenne pepper (if using), and salt. Pulse until the mixture is coarse but not smooth.
2. Transfer the mixture to a bowl. Add flour and baking powder, then mix until well combined. The mixture should be firm enough to shape into balls.
3. Heat vegetable oil in a frying pan over medium heat.
4. Form the chickpea mixture into small balls or patties.
5. Carefully place the falafel into the hot oil and fry until golden brown and crispy, about 3-4 minutes per side.
6. Remove the falafel from the oil and drain on paper towels to remove excess oil.

Nutritional Information (per serving): 250 calories, 10g protein, 35g carbohydrates, 8g fat, 7g fiber, 0mg cholesterol, 400mg sodium, 450mg potassium.

LENTIL STUFFED PEPPERS

INGREDIENTS

2
15 mins
40 mins

- 2 large bell peppers, halved and seeds removed
- 1/2 cup dry green lentils; 1 cup vegetable broth
- 1/2 small onion, finely chopped
- 1 clove garlic, minced
- 1/2 cup diced tomatoes (canned or fresh)
- 1/2 tsp ground cumin; 1/2 tsp paprika
- Salt and pepper to taste
- 1/4 cup shredded mozzarella cheese (optional)
- Fresh parsley, chopped (for garnish)

DIRECTIONS

1. Preheat the oven to 375°F (190°C). Place the halved bell peppers in a baking dish, cut side up.
2. Rinse the lentils under cold water and drain. Combine the lentils and vegetable broth in a saucepan. Bring to a boil, then reduce heat and simmer for 15-20 minutes, or until the lentils are tender and most liquid is absorbed.
3. Heat olive oil over medium heat in a separate skillet. Add the chopped onion and garlic, and sauté until softened.
4. Add the diced tomatoes, ground cumin, paprika, salt, and pepper to the skillet. Stir well and cook for another 5 minutes.
5. Combine the cooked lentils with the tomato mixture in the skillet. Stir to combine and adjust the seasoning if needed.
6. Spoon the lentil mixture into the halved bell peppers, filling them evenly.
7. If using, sprinkle shredded mozzarella cheese on top of each stuffed pepper.
8. Cover the baking dish with foil and bake for 25-30 minutes or until the peppers are tender.
9. Garnish with fresh chopped parsley before serving.

Nutritional Information (per serving): 320 calories, 15g protein, 50g carbohydrates, 5g fat, 15g fiber, 0mg cholesterol, 700mg sodium, 900mg potassium.

• PIZZA •

FOUR CHEESE PIZZA

INGREDIENTS

2

15 mins
15 mins

- 1 pre-made whole wheat pizza crust (10-inch size)
- 1/2 cup tomato sauce; 1/4 cup crumbled feta cheese
- 1/4 cup fresh mozzarella cheese, sliced
- 1/4 cup ricotta cheese; 1/4 cup grated Parmesan cheese
- 1/2 cup spinach leaves, fresh
- 1 small zucchini, thinly sliced
- Olive oil; Salt and pepper to taste
- Fresh oregano or basil for garnish

DIRECTIONS

1. Preheat your oven to 450°F (230°C).
2. Place the pre-made whole wheat pizza crust on a baking sheet or pizza stone.
3. Spread the tomato sauce evenly over the crust, leaving a small border around the edges.
4. The crumbled feta, sliced mozzarella, dollops of ricotta, and grated Parmesan evenly over the sauce.
5. Arrange the fresh spinach leaves and sliced zucchini on the cheese.
6. Drizzle olive oil over the toppings and season with salt and pepper to taste.
7. Bake the pizza in the oven for about 12-15 minutes, until the crust is golden and the cheese is melted and bubbly. Remove the pizza from the oven and garnish with fresh oregano or basil before serving.

Nutritional Information (per serving): 360 calories, 16g protein, 38g carbohydrates, 18g fat, 3g fiber, 30mg cholesterol, 620mg sodium, 400mg potassium.

MEDITERRANEAN VEGGIE PIZZA

INGREDIENTS

2

15 mins

15 mins

- 1 premade pizza crust (10inch size)
- 1/2 cup tomato sauce
- 1 cup shredded mozzarella cheese
- 1/2 cup sliced bell peppers (assorted colors)
- 1/2 cup sliced red onions; 1/4 cup sliced black olives
- 1/4 cup crumbled feta cheese
- Fresh basil leaves
- Olive oil; Salt and pepper to taste

DIRECTIONS

1. Preheat your oven to 450°F (230°C).
2. Place the premade pizza crust on a baking sheet or pizza stone.
3. Spread the tomato sauce evenly over the crust, leaving a small border around the edges.
4. Sprinkle the shredded mozzarella cheese evenly over the sauce.
5. Arrange the sliced bell peppers, red onions, and black olives on the cheese.
6. Sprinkle the crumbled feta cheese over the vegetables.
7. Drizzle olive oil over the pizza and season with salt and pepper to taste.
8. Bake the pizza in the oven for about 12-15 minutes, until the crust is golden and the cheese is melted and bubbly. Remove the pizza from the oven and garnish with fresh basil leaves before serving.

Nutritional Information (per serving): 320 calories, 14g protein, 40g carbohydrates, 12g fat, 3g fiber, 25mg cholesterol, 700mg sodium, 350mg potassium.

GREEK PIZZA

INGREDIENTS

- 1 premade pizza crust (10inch size)
- 1/2 cup tomato sauce
- 1 cup shredded mozzarella cheese
- 1/2 cup diced tomatoes
- 1/4 cup sliced black olives
- 1/4 cup crumbled feta cheese
- 1/4 cup chopped red onions
- Fresh basil leaves
- Olive oil
- Salt and pepper to taste
- Optional: sliced gyro meat or grilled chicken for protein

2

15 mins

15 mins

DIRECTIONS

1. Preheat your oven to 450°F (230°C).
2. Place the premade pizza crust on a baking sheet or pizza stone.
3. Spread the tomato sauce evenly over the crust, leaving a small border around the edges.
4. Sprinkle the shredded mozzarella cheese evenly over the sauce.
5. Scatter the diced tomatoes, black olives, crumbled feta cheese, and chopped red onions over the cheese.
6. Add sliced gyro meat or grilled chicken to the vegetables.
7. Drizzle olive oil over the pizza and season with salt and pepper to taste.
8. Bake the pizza in the oven for about 12-15 minutes, until the crust is golden and the cheese is melted and bubbly.
9. Remove the pizza from the oven and garnish with fresh basil leaves before serving.

Nutritional Information (per serving): 350 calories, 16g protein, 35g carbohydrates, 16g fat, 3g fiber, 30mg cholesterol, 650mg sodium, 320mg potassium.

CAPRESE PIZZA

INGREDIENTS

2

15 mins

15 mins

- 1 premade pizza crust (10inch size)
- 1/2 cup tomato sauce
- 1 cup shredded mozzarella cheese
- 1 large tomato, thinly sliced
- 1/2 cup fresh basil leaves
- 2 tablespoons balsamic glaze
- Salt and pepper to taste
- Olive oil

DIRECTIONS

1. Preheat your oven to 450°F (230°C).
2. Place the premade pizza crust on a baking sheet or pizza stone.
3. Spread the tomato sauce evenly over the crust, leaving a small border around the edges.
4. Sprinkle the shredded mozzarella cheese evenly over the sauce.
5. Arrange the tomato slices on top of the cheese.
6. Tear the fresh basil leaves and scatter them over the pizza.
7. Drizzle olive oil over the pizza and season with salt and pepper to taste.
8. Bake the pizza in the oven for about 12-15 minutes, until the crust is golden and the cheese is melted and bubbly. Remove the pizza from the oven and drizzle with balsamic glaze before serving.

Nutritional Information (per serving): 320 calories, 14g protein, 30g carbohydrates, 16g fat, 2g fiber, 25mg cholesterol, 600mg sodium, 280mg potassium.

MEDITERRANEAN CHICKEN PIZZA

INGREDIENTS

- 1 premade pizza crust (10inch size)
- 1/2 cup marinara sauce
- 1 cup cooked chicken breast, shredded
- 1/2 cup sliced black olives
- 1/2 cup diced red bell pepper
- 1/2 cup crumbled feta cheese
- 1/4 cup chopped fresh parsley
- 1 teaspoon dried oregano
- Salt and pepper to taste
- Olive oil

2

15 mins

20 mins

DIRECTIONS

1. Preheat your oven to 450°F (230°C).
2. Place the premade pizza crust on a baking sheet or pizza stone.
3. Spread the marinara sauce evenly over the crust, leaving a small border around the edges.
4. Scatter the shredded chicken, black olives, and diced red bell pepper over the sauce.
5. Sprinkle the crumbled feta cheese, chopped fresh parsley, and dried oregano over the pizza.
6. Drizzle olive oil over the pizza and season with salt and pepper to taste.
7. Bake the pizza in the oven for about 12-15 minutes, until the crust is golden and the cheese is melted and bubbly.
8. Remove the pizza from the oven and let it cool slightly before slicing and serving.

Nutritional Information (per serving): 380 calories, 24g protein, 38g carbohydrates, 14g fat, 3g fiber, 50mg cholesterol, 820mg sodium, 320mg potassium.

MUSHROOM AND ARUGULA PIZZA

INGREDIENTS

2

15 mins

15 mins

- 1 premade pizza crust (10inch size)
- 1/2 cup marinara sauce
- 1 cup sliced mushrooms
- 1 cup fresh arugula
- 1/2 cup shredded mozzarella cheese
- 1/4 cup grated Parmesan cheese
- 2 cloves garlic, minced
- Olive oil
- Salt and pepper to taste
- Red pepper flakes (optional)

DIRECTIONS

1. Preheat your oven to 450°F (230°C).
2. Place the premade pizza crust on a baking sheet or pizza stone.
3. Spread the marinara sauce evenly over the crust, leaving a small border around the edges.
4. Scatter the sliced mushrooms and minced garlic over the sauce.
5. Sprinkle the shredded mozzarella cheese and grated Parmesan cheese over the pizza.
6. Drizzle olive oil over the pizza and season with salt, pepper, and red pepper flakes (if using).
7. Bake the pizza in the oven for about 12-15 minutes, until the crust is golden and the cheese is melted and bubbly. Remove the pizza from the oven and top with fresh arugula. Slice and serve immediately.

Nutritional Information (per serving): 320 calories, 14g protein, 38g carbohydrates, 12g fat, 3g fiber, 20mg cholesterol, 640mg sodium, 320mg potassium.

SPINACH AND RICOTTA PIZZA

INGREDIENTS

2

15 mins

15 mins

- 1 premade pizza crust (10inch size)
- 1/2 cup marinara sauce
- 1 cup fresh spinach leaves
- 1/2 cup ricotta cheese
- 1/4 cup grated Parmesan cheese
- 2 cloves garlic, minced
- Olive oil
- Salt and pepper to taste
- Red pepper flakes (optional)

DIRECTIONS

1. Preheat your oven to 450°F (230°C).
2. Place the premade pizza crust on a baking sheet or pizza stone.
3. Spread the marinara sauce evenly over the crust, leaving a small border around the edges.
4. Scatter the fresh spinach leaves and minced garlic over the sauce.
5. Drop spoonfuls of ricotta cheese evenly over the pizza.
6. Sprinkle grated Parmesan cheese on top of the ricotta.
7. Drizzle olive oil over the pizza and season with salt, pepper, and red pepper flakes (if using).
8. Bake the pizza in the oven for about 12-15 minutes, until the crust is golden and the cheese is melted and bubbly. Remove the pizza from the oven, slice, and serve hot.

Nutritional Information (per serving): 340 calories, 15g protein, 38g carbohydrates, 14g fat, 3g fiber, 25mg cholesterol, 660mg sodium, 360mg potassium.

MEDITERRANEAN SEAFOOD PIZZA

INGREDIENTS

2

15 mins

15 mins

- 1 premade pizza crust (10inch size)
- 1/2 cup marinara sauce
- 4 oz cooked shrimp, peeled and deveined
- 4 oz cooked crab meat; 1/4 cup sliced black olives
- 1/4 cup diced red onion
- 1/2 cup crumbled feta cheese
- 2 tbsp chopped fresh parsley
- Olive oil; Salt and pepper to taste
- Red pepper flakes (optional)

DIRECTIONS

1. Preheat your oven to 450°F (230°C).
2. Place the premade pizza crust on a baking sheet or pizza stone.
3. Spread the marinara sauce evenly over the crust, leaving a small border around the edges.
4. Arrange the cooked shrimp and crab meat in the sauce.
5. Scatter sliced black olives and diced red onion over the seafood.
6. Sprinkle crumbled feta cheese and chopped fresh parsley evenly over the pizza.
7. Drizzle olive oil over the pizza and season with salt, pepper, and red pepper flakes (if using).
8. Bake the pizza in the oven for about 12-15 minutes, until the crust is golden and the cheese is melted and bubbly. Remove the pizza from the oven, slice, and serve hot.

Nutritional Information (per serving): 410 calories, 24g protein, 35g carbohydrates, 18g fat, 3g fiber, 140mg cholesterol, 960mg sodium, 370mg potassium.

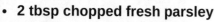

EGGPLANT AND GOAT CHEESE PIZZA

INGREDIENTS

2

20 mins

15 mins

- 1 premade pizza crust (10inch size)
- 1 small eggplant, thinly sliced
- 2 tbsp olive oil
- Salt and pepper to taste
- 1/2 cup marinara sauce
- 4 oz goat cheese, crumbled
- 1/4 cup sliced cherry tomatoes
- 2 tbsp chopped fresh basil
- Red pepper flakes (optional)

DIRECTIONS

1. Preheat your oven to 450°F (230°C).
2. Place the thinly sliced eggplant on a baking sheet, drizzle with olive oil, and season with salt and pepper. Roast in the preheated oven for about
10-12 minutes until tender.
3. Spread marinara sauce evenly over the premade pizza crust.
4. Arrange the roasted eggplant slices on top of the sauce.
5. Scatter crumbled goat cheese and sliced cherry tomatoes over the pizza.
6. Sprinkle chopped fresh basil and red pepper flakes (if using) on top.
7. Bake the pizza in the oven for about 12-15 minutes or until the crust is golden and the cheese is melted. Remove from the oven, slice, and serve hot.

Nutritional Information (per serving): 410 calories, 14g protein, 38g carbohydrates, 23g fat, 5g fiber, 15mg cholesterol, 690mg sodium, 480mg potassium.

SUNDRIED TOMATO AND OLIVE PIZZA

INGREDIENTS

2

15 mins

15 mins

- 1 premade pizza crust (10inch size)
- 1/4 cup sundried tomatoes, chopped
- 1/4 cup sliced black olives
- 1/4 cup crumbled feta cheese
- 2 tbsp olive oil; 2 garlic cloves, minced
- 1/2 tsp dried oregano
- Salt and pepper to taste;
- Red pepper flakes (optional)
- Fresh basil leaves for garnish

DIRECTIONS

1. Preheat your oven to 450°F (230°C).
2. Mix the chopped sundried tomatoes, sliced black olives, crumbled feta cheese, minced garlic, olive oil, dried oregano, salt, and pepper in a small bowl.
3. Spread this mixture evenly over the premade pizza crust.
4. Optionally, sprinkle some red pepper flakes for added heat.
5. Bake the pizza in the oven for about 12-15 minutes or until the crust is golden and the cheese is melted. Remove from the oven, garnish with fresh basil leaves, slice, and serve hot.

Nutritional Information (per serving): 420 calories, 10g protein, 42g carbohydrates, 24g fat, 4g fiber, 20mg cholesterol, 820mg sodium, 360mg potassium.

MEDITERRANEAN SHRIMP PIZZA

INGREDIENTS

2

15 mins

15 mins

- 1 premade pizza crust (10inch size)
- 8 oz shrimp, peeled and deveined
- 1/4 cup sliced Kalamata olives
- 1/4 cup diced red bell pepper
- 1/4 cup crumbled feta cheese
- 2 tbsp olive oil
- 2 garlic cloves, minced
- 1 tsp dried oregano
- Salt and pepper to taste
- Fresh parsley for garnish

DIRECTIONS

1. Preheat your oven to 450°F (230°C).

2. In a skillet, heat olive oil over medium heat. Add minced garlic and sauté until fragrant.

3. Add shrimp to the skillet and cook until they turn pink and opaque, about 2-3 minutes per side—season with salt, pepper, and dried oregano.

4. Place the premade pizza crust on a baking sheet.

5. Spread the cooked shrimp evenly over the pizza crust—top with sliced olives, diced red bell pepper, and crumbled feta cheese.

6. Bake the pizza in the oven for about 12-15 minutes or until the crust is golden and the cheese is melted. Remove from the oven, garnish with fresh parsley, slice, and serve hot.

Nutritional Information (per serving): 430 calories, 30g protein, 35g carbohydrates, 20g fat, 4g fiber, 180mg cholesterol, 920mg sodium, 320mg potassium.

PROSCIUTTO PIZZA

INGREDIENTS

2

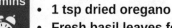
15 mins

15 mins

- 1 premade pizza crust (10inch size)
- 4 oz prosciutto, thinly sliced
- 1 cup shredded mozzarella cheese
- 1/4 cup grated Parmesan cheese
- 1/4 cup tomato sauce
- 1 tbsp olive oil
- 1 tsp dried oregano
- Fresh basil leaves for garnish
- Red pepper flakes (optional)
- Salt and pepper to taste

DIRECTIONS

1. Preheat your oven to 450°F (230°C).

2. Place the premade pizza crust on a baking sheet.

3. Spread tomato sauce evenly over the pizza crust, leaving a small border around the edges.

4. Sprinkle shredded mozzarella cheese and grated Parmesan cheese over the tomato sauce.

5. Arrange the thinly sliced prosciutto on top of the cheese.

6. Drizzle olive oil over the pizza and sprinkle dried oregano, salt, and pepper.

7. Optionally, add red pepper flakes for a bit of heat.

8. Bake the pizza in the oven for about 12-15 minutes or until the crust is golden and the cheese is bubbly and melted. Remove from the oven, garnish with fresh basil leaves, slice, and serve hot.

Nutritional Information (per serving): 550 calories, 30g protein, 35g carbohydrates, 30g fat, 2g fiber, 90mg cholesterol, 1240mg sodium, 280mg potassium.

MEDITERRANEAN VEGETABLE STEW

INGREDIENTS

- 1 zucchini, diced
- 1 yellow bell pepper, diced
- 1 red onion, chopped; 2 cloves garlic, minced
- 1 can (14 oz) diced tomatoes, with juices
- 1 can (15 oz) chickpeas, drained and rinsed
- 1 cup vegetable broth
- 1 tsp dried oregano, 1 tsp dried basil
- Salt and pepper to taste; 2 tbsp olive oil

2

10 mins

25 mins

DIRECTIONS

1. Heat olive oil over medium heat in a large pot. Add chopped red onion and minced garlic, and sauté until fragrant.
2. Add diced eggplant, zucchini, and yellow bell pepper to the pot. Season with dried oregano, dried basil, salt, and pepper. Cook for about 5 minutes until the vegetables start to soften.
3. Pour in diced tomatoes with their juices and vegetable broth. Stir well to combine.
4. Cover the pot and let the stew simmer for 15-20 minutes or until the vegetables are tender.
5. Add chickpeas to the stew and cook for 5 minutes to heat through.
6. Taste and adjust seasoning if needed. Remove from heat.
7. Serve the Mediterranean vegetable stew hot, garnished with fresh parsley.

Nutritional Information (per serving): 320 calories, 12g protein, 50g carbohydrates, 10g fat, 12g fiber, 0mg cholesterol, 680mg sodium, 980mg potassium.

SPINACH AND FETA PITA BAKE

INGREDIENTS

2

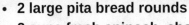

15 mins

20 mins

- 2 large pita bread rounds
- 2 cups fresh spinach, chopped
- 1/2 cup crumbled feta cheese
- 1/4 cup diced red onion
- 2 tbsp olive oil
- 1 tsp dried oregano
- Salt and pepper to taste

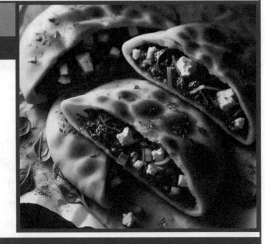

DIRECTIONS

1. Preheat your oven to 375°F (190°C).
2. Cut each pita bread round in half to form pockets.
3. Mix together chopped spinach, crumbled feta cheese, diced red onion, olive oil, dried oregano, salt, and pepper in a bowl.
4. Stuff each pita pocket with the spinach and feta mixture.
5. Place the stuffed pitas on a baking sheet lined with parchment paper.
6. Bake in the oven for 15-20 minutes or until the pita bread is crispy and the filling is heated.
7. Remove from the oven and let cool slightly before serving.

Nutritional Information (per serving): 320 calories, 12g protein, 35g carbohydrates, 15g fat, 5g fiber, 15mg cholesterol, 580mg sodium, 420mg potassium.

MEDITERRANEAN VEGETABLE CAKES

INGREDIENTS

2

20 mins

15 mins

- 1 cup grated zucchini
- 1 cup grated carrots
- 1/2 cup cooked quinoa
- 1/4 cup chopped fresh parsley
- 1/4 cup crumbled feta cheese
- 1/4 cup breadcrumbs; 1 egg
- 1 clove garlic, minced
- 1 tsp dried oregano
- Salt and pepper to taste; Olive oil for frying

DIRECTIONS

1. In a large bowl, combine grated zucchini, grated carrots, cooked quinoa, chopped parsley, crumbled feta cheese, breadcrumbs, egg, minced garlic, dried oregano, salt, and pepper. Mix until well combined.

2. Heat olive oil in a skillet over medium heat.

3. Form the vegetable mixture into patties and carefully place them in the hot skillet.

4. Cook the vegetable cakes for 3-4 minutes on each side or until golden brown is cooked.

5. Transfer the vegetable cakes to a plate lined with paper towels to absorb excess oil once cooked.

6. Warm the Mediterranean vegetable cakes with a side of Greek yogurt or tzatziki sauce, if desired.

Nutritional Information (per serving): 180 calories, 4g protein, 20g carbohydrates, 10g fat, 7g fiber, 0mg cholesterol, 300mg sodium, 800mg potassium.

RICE SALAD WITH VEGETABLES

INGREDIENTS

2

15 mins

15 mins

- 1/2 cup long-grain white rice; 1 cup water
- 1/2 cup cherry tomatoes, halved
- 1/2 cup cucumber, diced
- 1/4 cup red onion, finely chopped
- 1/4 cup Kalamata olives, pitted and sliced
- 1/4 cup feta cheese, crumbled
- 2 tbsp fresh parsley, chopped; 2 tbsp olive oil
- 1 tbsp lemon juice; Salt and pepper to taste

DIRECTIONS

1. Combine the white rice and water in a medium saucepan. Bring to a boil, then reduce heat to low, cover, and simmer for 15 minutes or until the rice is tender and the water is absorbed. Remove from heat and let it cool slightly.

2. In a large mixing bowl, combine the cooked rice, halved cherry tomatoes, diced cucumber, finely chopped red onion, sliced Kalamata olives, crumbled feta cheese, and chopped parsley.

3. Whisk the olive oil, lemon juice, salt, and pepper in a small bowl to make the dressing.

4. Pour the dressing over the rice and vegetable mixture, then toss gently to coat everything evenly.

5. Immediately serve the Mediterranean rice salad as a light, refreshing meal or side dish.

Nutritional Information (per serving): 320 calories, 7g protein, 38g carbohydrates, 16g fat, 3g fiber, 10mg cholesterol, 350mg sodium, 280mg potassium.

ZUCCHINI NOODLES WITH PESTO

INGREDIENTS

- 2 medium zucchinis, spiralized into noodles
- 1 cup cherry tomatoes, halved
- 1/4 cup basil pesto (store-bought or homemade)
- 1 tbsp olive oil
- 1/4 cup grated Parmesan cheese (optional)
- Salt and pepper to taste
- Fresh basil leaves for garnish (optional)

2

10 mins

5 mins

DIRECTIONS

1. Heat the olive oil over medium heat in a large skillet.
2. Add the spiralized zucchini noodles to the skillet and sauté for 2-3 minutes, stirring gently until they are slightly softened but still have a bit of crunch.
3. Add the halved cherry tomatoes to the skillet and cook for an additional 1-2 minutes until warmed through.
4. Remove the skillet from heat and stir in the basil pesto, mixing until the noodles and tomatoes are well coated.
5. Season with salt and pepper to taste. If desired, sprinkle with grated Parmesan cheese before serving. If desired, garnish with fresh basil leaves and serve immediately.

Nutritional Information (per serving): 210 calories, 6g protein, 10g carbohydrates, 16g fat, 4g fiber, 5mg cholesterol, 150mg sodium, 500mg potassium.

ITALIAN GRILLED EGGPLANT WITH BASIL AND PARSLEY

INGREDIENTS

2

10 mins

10 mins

- 1 medium eggplant, sliced into rounds
- 2 tbsp olive oil
- Salt and pepper to taste
- 2 tbsp fresh basil, chopped
- 2 tbsp fresh parsley, chopped
- 1 clove garlic, minced
- 1 tbsp lemon juice

DIRECTIONS

1. Preheat a grill or grill pan over medium-high heat.
2. Brush both sides of the eggplant slices with olive oil and season with salt and pepper.
3. Grill the eggplant slices for 4-5 minutes per side or until tender and grill marks appear.
4. Mix the chopped basil, parsley, minced garlic, and lemon juice in a small bowl to make a dressing.
5. Arrange the grilled eggplant slices on a serving plate and drizzle the herb dressing.
6. Serve the Italian grilled eggplant as a delicious appetizer or side dish.

Nutritional Information (per serving): 180 calories, 2g protein, 14g carbohydrates, 14g fat, 6g fiber, 0mg cholesterol, 200mg sodium, 420mg potassium.

MEDITERRANEAN VEGGIE WRAPS

INGREDIENTS

- 4 whole wheat tortillas; 1 cup hummus
- 1 cup mixed salad greens
- 1/2 cup cherry tomatoes, halved
- 1/2 cup cucumber, sliced
- 1/4 cup red onion, thinly sliced
- 1/4 cup Kalamata olives, sliced
- 1/4 cup crumbled feta cheese
- Fresh lemon juice for drizzling
- Salt and pepper to taste

2

15 mins

0 mins

DIRECTIONS

1. Lay out the whole wheat tortillas on a clean surface.
2. Spread 1/4 cup of hummus evenly onto each tortilla.
3. Divide the mixed salad greens, cherry tomatoes, cucumber, red onion, Kalamata olives, and feta cheese among the tortillas.
4. Drizzle fresh lemon juice over the veggies and season with salt and pepper to taste.
5. Roll up each tortilla tightly into a wrap.
6. Slice the wraps in half diagonally and serve immediately.

Nutritional Information (per serving): 320 calories, 10g protein, 45g carbohydrates, 12g fat, 8g fiber, 10mg cholesterol, 500mg sodium, 400mg potassium.

EGGPLANT PARMESAN

INGREDIENTS

2

20 mins

40 mins

- 1 large eggplant, sliced into 1/2inch rounds
- 1 cup marinara sauce
- 1/2 cup shredded mozzarella cheese
- 1/4 cup grated Parmesan cheese
- 1/4 cup breadcrumbs
- 1/4 cup chopped fresh basil
- 1/4 teaspoon dried oregano
- Salt and pepper to taste
- Olive oil for brushing

DIRECTIONS

1. Preheat the oven to 400°F (200°C). Lightly grease a baking sheet with olive oil.
2. Arrange the eggplant slices on the baking sheet. Brush both sides of the eggplant slices with olive oil and season with salt and pepper. Bake the eggplant slices for about 20 minutes, flipping halfway through, until they are tender and lightly browned. Remove the eggplant slices from the oven and reduce the temperature to 350°F (175°C).
3. Mix the breadcrumbs, Parmesan cheese, and dried oregano in a small bowl.
4. Spread a thin layer of marinara sauce in a baking dish. Arrange half of the baked eggplant slices on top of the sauce.
5. Sprinkle half of the breadcrumb mixture over the eggplant slices, followed by half of the shredded mozzarella cheese.
6. Repeat the layers with the remaining eggplant slices, breadcrumb mixture, and mozzarella cheese.
7. Bake the Eggplant Parmesan in the oven for about 20 minutes or until the cheese is melted and bubbly.
8. Garnish with chopped fresh basil before serving.

Nutritional Information (per serving): 350 calories, 15g protein, 30g carbohydrates, 20g fat, 8g fiber, 25mg cholesterol, 700mg sodium, 800mg potassium.

FALAFEL PITA SANDWICHES

INGREDIENTS

- 1 cup cooked chickpeas (garbanzo beans), drained and rinsed
- 1/4 cup finely chopped onion; 2 cloves garlic, minced
- 2 tablespoons chopped fresh parsley;
- 1 teaspoon ground cumin
- 1/2 teaspoon ground coriander; 1/4 teaspoon baking powder
- Salt and pepper to taste
- 2 tablespoons all-purpose flour; 2 tablespoons olive oil
- 2 whole wheat pita bread
- Toppings: shredded lettuce, sliced tomatoes, cucumber, tahini sauce, hot sauce (opc)

2

20 mins

15 mins

DIRECTIONS

1. In a food processor, combine the chickpeas, onion, garlic, parsley, cumin, coriander, baking powder, salt, and pepper. Pulse until the mixture is finely chopped but not completely smooth.
2. Transfer the mixture to a bowl. Add the flour and mix until well combined. The mixture should hold together when shaped into small balls. If it's too dry, you can add a little water.
3. Shape the falafel mixture into small patties or balls about 1 inch in diameter.
4. Heat the olive oil in a skillet over medium heat. Cook the falafel patties on each side for 3-4 minutes or until golden brown and crispy.
5. Warm the pita bread in a toaster or oven while the falafel cooks.
6. To assemble the sandwiches, cut the pita bread in half to form pockets. Stuff each pita pocket with shredded lettuce, sliced tomatoes, cucumber, and 3 to 4 falafel patties. Drizzle with tahini sauce and hot sauce, if desired.
7. Serve the falafel pita sandwiches immediately.

Nutritional Information (per serving): 350 calories, 10g protein, 50g carbohydrates, 12g fat, 8g fiber, 0mg cholesterol, 600mg sodium, 400mg potassium.

MUSHROOM RISOTTO

INGREDIENTS

2

10 mins

25 mins

- 1 cup arborio rice
- 2 cups vegetable broth
- 1 cup sliced mushrooms
- 1/2 onion, finely chopped
- 2 cloves garlic, minced
- 1/4 cup dry white wine (optional)
- 2 tablespoons olive oil
- 2 tablespoons grated Parmesan cheese
- Salt and pepper to taste
- Fresh parsley for garnish

DIRECTIONS

1. In a saucepan, heat the vegetable broth over low heat until warm.
2. Heat the olive oil over medium heat in a separate large skillet. Add the chopped onion and sauté until translucent, about 3-4 minutes.
3. Add the minced garlic and sliced mushrooms to the skillet. Cook until the mushrooms are tender and golden brown, about 5-6 minutes. Stir in the arborio rice and cook for 1-2 minutes until the rice is lightly toasted.
4. Begin adding the warm vegetable broth to the skillet, about 1/2 cup at a time, stirring frequently. Allow the broth to be absorbed by the rice before adding more. Continue this process until the rice is creamy and cooked al dente, about 20-25 minutes. Stir in the grated Parmesan cheese and season with salt and pepper to taste.
5. Remove the skillet from heat and let the risotto rest for a few minutes. Serve the mushroom risotto garnished with fresh parsley.

Nutritional Information (per serving): 400 calories, 8g protein, 65g carbohydrates, 12g fat, 4g fiber, 5mg cholesterol, 800mg sodium, 250mg potassium.

PASTA PRIMAVERA

INGREDIENTS

- 6 oz pasta (such as spaghetti or fettuccine)
- 1 cup cherry tomatoes, halved
- 1/2 cup bell peppers, sliced
- 1/2 cup zucchini, sliced
- 1/2 cup broccoli florets
- 2 cloves garlic, minced
- 2 tablespoons olive oil
- Salt and pepper to taste
- 2 tablespoons grated Parmesan cheese
- Fresh basil leaves for garnish

2

10 mins

15 mins

DIRECTIONS

1. Cook the pasta according to package instructions until al dente. Drain and set aside.
2. Heat the olive oil in a large skillet over medium heat. Add the minced garlic and sauté until fragrant, about 1 minute.
3. Add the cherry tomatoes, bell peppers, zucchini, and broccoli to the skillet. Sauté until the vegetables are tender yet still crisp, about 5-6 minutes.
4. Season the vegetables with salt and pepper to taste.
5. Add the cooked pasta to the skillet with the vegetables. Toss everything together until well combined and heated through about 2-3 minutes.
6. Remove the skillet from heat and sprinkle grated Parmesan cheese over the pasta primavera.
7. Serve the pasta primavera garnished with fresh basil leaves.

Nutritional Information (per serving): 400 calories, 12g protein, 60g carbohydrates, 14g fat, 5g fiber, 5mg cholesterol, 300mg sodium, 450mg potassium.

SPANAKOPITA (GREEK SPINACH PIE)

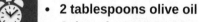

INGREDIENTS

2

20 mins

40 mins

- 6 sheets of phyllo dough
- 1 pound fresh spinach, chopped
- 1/2 cup feta cheese, crumbled
- 1/4 cup grated Parmesan cheese
- 1/4 cup chopped fresh dill
- 1/4 cup chopped fresh parsley
- 1/4 cup chopped green onions
- 2 tablespoons olive oil
- Salt and pepper to taste
- Nonstick cooking spray

DIRECTIONS

1. Preheat your oven to 375°F (190°C). Grease a baking dish with nonstick cooking spray.
2. Heat olive oil over medium heat in a large skillet. Add the chopped spinach and cook until wilted, about 5-7 minutes. Remove from heat and let it cool.
3. In a mixing bowl, combine the cooked spinach, crumbled feta cheese, grated Parmesan cheese, chopped dill, parsley, green onions, salt, and pepper. Mix well.
4. Lay one sheet of phyllo dough in the prepared baking dish. Lightly brush it with olive oil. Repeat with five more sheets of phyllo dough, brushing each layer with olive oil.
5. Spread the spinach and cheese mixture evenly over the phyllo dough layers in the baking dish.
6. Fold the edges of the phyllo dough over the spinach mixture to cover it completely. Lightly brush the top of the pie with olive oil.
7. Bake in the oven for 30-35 minutes or until the phyllo dough is golden brown and crispy.
8. Remove from the oven and let it cool for a few minutes before slicing and serving.

Nutritional Information (per serving): 350 calories, 12g protein, 25g carbohydrates, 22g fat, 4g fiber, 35mg cholesterol, 550mg sodium, 800mg potassium.

• PASTA •

WHOLE WHEAT SPAGHETTI WITH CHERRY TOMATOES

INGREDIENTS

- 6 ounces whole wheat spaghetti
- 1 cup cherry tomatoes, halved
- 2 cloves garlic, minced
- 2 tablespoons olive oil
- 1/4 teaspoon red pepper flakes (optional)
- Salt and pepper to taste
- Fresh basil leaves for garnish
- Grated Parmesan cheese for serving (optional)

2

10 mins

15 mins

DIRECTIONS

1. Cook the whole wheat spaghetti according to the package instructions until al dente. Drain and set aside.
2. Heat the olive oil in a large skillet over medium heat. Add the minced garlic and red pepper flakes (if using) and sauté for about 1 minute until fragrant.
3. Add the cherry tomatoes to the skillet and cook for 5-7 minutes, stirring occasionally, until they soften and release their juices. Season the tomato mixture with salt and pepper to taste.
4. Add the cooked spaghetti to the skillet with the tomato mixture. Toss everything together until the spaghetti is well coated with the tomato sauce. Cook for 2-3 minutes, allowing the flavors to meld together.
5. Remove from heat and garnish with fresh basil leaves.
6. Serve the whole wheat spaghetti with cherry tomatoes hot, topped with grated Parmesan cheese if desired.

Nutritional Information (per serving): 320 calories, 9g protein, 48g carbohydrates, 11g fat, 8g fiber, 0mg cholesterol, 150mg sodium, 300mg potassium.

PENNE WITH SPINACH PESTO

INGREDIENTS

2

15 mins

15 mins

- 6 ounces of penne pasta
- 2 cups fresh spinach leaves
- 1/4 cup fresh basil leaves
- 2 cloves garlic, minced
- 1/4 cup grated Parmesan cheese
- 1/4 cup pine nuts
- 1/4 cup olive oil
- Salt and pepper to taste
- Additional Parmesan cheese for serving (optional)

DIRECTIONS

1. Cook the penne pasta according to the package instructions until al dente. Drain and set aside.
2. Combine the fresh spinach, basil leaves, minced garlic, grated Parmesan cheese, pine nuts, and olive oil in a food processor. Process until smooth and well combined.
3. Season the spinach pesto with salt and pepper to taste. Adjust the consistency by adding more olive oil if needed. Heat the spinach pesto over medium heat for about 2 minutes in a large skillet.
4. Add the cooked penne pasta to the skillet with the spinach pesto. Toss everything together until the pasta is evenly coated with the pesto sauce.
5. Cook for an additional 2-3 minutes, stirring occasionally, to heat through.
6. Serve the penne with spinach pesto hot, garnished with additional grated Parmesan cheese if desired.

Nutritional Information (per serving): 480 calories, 14g protein, 47g carbohydrates, 27g fat, 4g fiber, 10mg cholesterol, 350mg sodium, 300mg potassium.

ORZO WITH ROASTED VEGETABLES

INGREDIENTS

- 1 cup orzo pasta
- 1 small zucchini, sliced
- 1 small yellow squash, sliced
- 1 red bell pepper, diced
- 1/2 red onion, sliced
- 2 tablespoons olive oil
- 2 cloves garlic, minced
- 1 teaspoon dried oregano
- Salt and pepper to taste
- Grated Parmesan cheese for serving (optional)

2

15 mins

20 mins

DIRECTIONS

1. Preheat your oven to 400°F (200°C). Line a baking sheet with parchment paper.
2. In a large bowl, toss the sliced zucchini, yellow squash, diced red bell pepper, sliced red onion with olive oil, minced garlic, dried oregano, salt, and pepper until well coated.
3. Spread the vegetables in a single layer on the prepared baking sheet. Roast in the oven for about 20 minutes or until the vegetables are tender and slightly caramelized.
4. While the vegetables are roasting, cook the orzo pasta according to the package instructions until al dente. Drain and set aside.
5. combine the cooked orzo pasta in a serving bowl once the vegetables are roasted. Toss gently to combine everything.
6. If desired, Serve the orzo with roasted vegetables, garnished with grated Parmesan cheese.

Nutritional Information (per serving): 380 calories, 10g protein, 54g carbohydrates, 14g fat, 6g fiber, 0mg cholesterol, 320mg sodium, 680mg potassium.

LEMON GARLIC PASTA WITH ASPARAGUS

INGREDIENTS

2

10 mins

15 mins

- 6 ounces (about 1 1/2 cups) penne pasta
- 1 bunch asparagus, trimmed and cut into bite-sized pieces
- 2 tablespoons olive oil
- 3 cloves garlic, minced
- Zest of 1 lemon
- Juice of 1/2 lemon
- Salt and pepper to taste
- Grated Parmesan cheese for serving (optional)
- Fresh parsley, chopped (for garnish)

DIRECTIONS

1. Cook the penne pasta in salted boiling water according to the package instructions until al dente. Drain and set aside.
2. Heat olive oil in a large skillet over medium heat while the pasta cooks. Add minced garlic and sauté until fragrant, about 1-2 minutes.
3. Add the asparagus pieces to the skillet and sauté for 5-7 minutes, or until tender but still slightly crisp.
4. Add cooked penne pasta to the skillet with asparagus. Pour lemon juice over the pasta and toss everything together to combine.
5. Add lemon zest, salt, and pepper to taste. Stir well to coat the pasta evenly with the lemon garlic sauce.
6. Serve the lemon garlic pasta with asparagus hot, garnished with grated Parmesan cheese and chopped fresh parsley if desired.

Nutritional Information (per serving): 380 calories, 12g protein, 58g carbohydrates, 12g fat, 4g fiber, 0mg cholesterol, 200mg sodium, 460mg potassium.

MEDITERRANEAN FARFALLE

INGREDIENTS

- 6 ounces farfalle pasta
- 1 tablespoon olive oil; 2 cloves garlic, minced
- 1/2 cup cherry tomatoes, halved
- 1/4 cup black olives, sliced
- 2 tablespoons capers, drained;
- 1/2 teaspoon dried oregano
- 1/4 teaspoon red pepper flakes (optional)
- Salt and black pepper to taste
- Fresh basil leaves, chopped (for garnish)
- Grated Parmesan cheese (optional)

2

10 mins

15 mins

DIRECTIONS

1. Cook farfalle pasta in salted boiling water according to package instructions until al dente. Drain and set aside.
2. Heat olive oil in a large skillet over medium heat. Add minced garlic and sauté until fragrant, about 1 minute.
3. Add cherry tomatoes, black olives, and capers to the skillet. Cook for 3-4 minutes until the tomatoes start to soften.
4. Stir in dried oregano and red pepper flakes (if using), and season with salt and black pepper to taste.
5. Add cooked farfalle pasta to the skillet and toss everything together until well combined and heated.
6. Serve the Mediterranean farfalle hot, garnished with chopped fresh basil leaves and grated Parmesan cheese if desired.

Nutritional Information (per serving): 380 calories, 10g protein, 60g carbohydrates, 10g fat, 5g fiber, 0mg cholesterol, 350mg sodium, 280mg potassium.

LINGUINE WITH CLAMS

INGREDIENTS

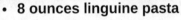

2

10 mins

15 mins

- 8 ounces linguine pasta
- 2 tablespoons olive oil
- 2 cloves garlic, minced
- 1/4 teaspoon red pepper flakes
- 1/2 cup dry white wine
- 1 pound littleneck clams, scrubbed
- 1/4 cup fresh parsley, chopped
- Salt and black pepper to taste
- Grated Parmesan cheese (optional for serving)

DIRECTIONS

1. Cook linguine pasta in a large pot of salted boiling water according to package instructions until al dente. Drain and set aside.
2. Heat olive oil over medium heat in a separate large skillet. Add minced garlic and red pepper flakes, sautéing until fragrant but not browned.
3. Pour in the white wine and bring to a simmer. Add the clams to the skillet, cover, and cook for about 5-7 minutes or until the clams have opened. Discard any unopened clams.
4. Add the cooked linguine pasta to the skillet with the clams and toss together gently to combine. Cook for an additional minute to let the flavors meld. Season with salt and black pepper to taste. Stir in chopped parsley. Serve the linguine with clams hot, garnished with grated Parmesan cheese if desired.

Nutritional Information (per serving): 550 calories, 25g protein, 70g carbohydrates, 18g fat, 3g fiber, 35mg cholesterol, 500mg sodium, 350mg potassium.

RATATOUILLE WITH PASTA

INGREDIENTS

- 4 ounces pasta (such as penne or fusilli)
- 2 tablespoons olive oil; 1 small onion, chopped
- 2 cloves garlic, minced
- 1 small eggplant, diced; 1 small zucchini, diced
- 1 small yellow squash, diced
- 1 red bell pepper, diced
- 1 can (14 ounces) diced tomatoes, drained
- 1 teaspoon dried basil; 1 teaspoon dried oregano
- Salt and black pepper to taste
- Grated Parmesan cheese (optional for serving)

2

15 mins

25 mins

DIRECTIONS

1. Cook pasta in a large pot of salted boiling water according to package instructions until al dente. Drain and set aside.

2. Heat olive oil over medium heat in a large skillet. Add chopped onion and minced garlic, sautéing until the onion is translucent and the garlic is fragrant.

3. Add diced eggplant, zucchini, yellow squash, and red bell pepper to the skillet. Cook, stirring occasionally, until vegetables are tender, about 10-12 minutes.

4. Stir in drained diced tomatoes, dried basil, and dried oregano—season with salt and black pepper to taste. Cook for an additional 5 minutes to let the flavors meld.

5. Add the cooked pasta to the skillet with the ratatouille mixture. Toss everything together gently to combine and heat through. Serve the ratatouille with pasta hot, garnished with grated Parmesan cheese if desired.

Nutritional Information (per serving): 450 calories, 10g protein, 70g carbohydrates, 15g fat, 8g fiber, 0mg cholesterol, 300mg sodium, 900mg potassium.

FUSILLI WITH KALE AND WALNUT PESTO

INGREDIENTS

2

10 mins

15 mins

- 4 ounces fusilli pasta
- 2 cups kale leaves, stems removed
- 1/4 cup walnuts
- 2 cloves garlic
- 2 tablespoons grated Parmesan cheese
- 2 tablespoons olive oil
- Salt and black pepper to taste
- Red pepper flakes (optional, for spice)

DIRECTIONS

1. Cook fusilli pasta in a large pot of salted boiling water according to package instructions until al dente. Drain and set aside, reserving some pasta water.

2. Combine kale leaves, walnuts, garlic, Parmesan cheese, olive oil, salt, black pepper, and red pepper flakes in a food processor. Pulse until ingredients are finely chopped and combined.

3. If the pesto is too thick, add some reserved pasta water to thin it out to your desired consistency.

4. Toss the cooked fusilli pasta with the kale and walnut pesto until well coated.

Serve the fusilli with kale and walnut pesto warm, garnished with additional grated Parmesan cheese if desired.

Nutritional Information (per serving): 500 calories, 14g protein, 55g carbohydrates, 25g fat, 7g fiber, 5mg cholesterol, 150mg sodium, 550mg potassium.

MUSHROOM AND SPINACH LASAGNA

INGREDIENTS

- 6 lasagna noodles
- 1 cup sliced mushrooms
- 1 cup fresh spinach leaves
- 1/2 cup ricotta cheese
- 1/2 cup shredded mozzarella cheese
- 1/4 cup grated Parmesan cheese
- 1 can (15 ounces) diced tomatoes, drained
- 1/2 teaspoon dried oregano; 1/2 teaspoon dried basil
- Salt and pepper to taste
- Olive oil for cooking

2

20 mins

40 mins

DIRECTIONS

1. Preheat your oven to 375°F (190°C).
2. Cook the lasagna noodles according to package instructions until al dente. Drain and set aside.
3. Heat olive oil over medium heat in a pan. Add sliced mushrooms and cook until tender, about 5 minutes.
4. Add fresh spinach to the pan and cook until wilted—season with salt and pepper.
5. In a bowl, combine ricotta cheese, shredded mozzarella cheese, grated Parmesan cheese, diced tomatoes, dried oregano, and dried basil. Mix well.
6. Layer the cooked lasagna noodles, mushroom and spinach, and cheese mixture in a baking dish. Repeat the layers until all ingredients are used, finishing with a layer of cheese on top.
7. Cover the baking dish with foil and bake in the oven for 25 minutes. Remove the foil and bake for 10-15 minutes until the cheese is bubbly and golden. Let the lasagna cool slightly before slicing and serving.

Nutritional Information (per serving): 480 calories, 22g protein, 52g carbohydrates, 20g fat, 4g fiber, 40mg cholesterol, 600mg sodium, 450mg potassium.

PESTO PASTA

INGREDIENTS

2

10 mins

10 mins

- 6 ounces whole wheat pasta
- 2 cups fresh basil leaves
- 1/4 cup grated Parmesan cheese
- 1/4 cup walnuts
- 2 cloves garlic
- 1/4 cup olive oil
- Salt and pepper to taste

DIRECTIONS

1. Cook the whole wheat pasta according to package instructions until al dente.
Drain and set aside.
2. Combine basil leaves, Parmesan cheese, walnuts, garlic, olive oil, salt, and pepper in a food processor. Blend until smooth to make the pesto sauce.
3. Heat the pesto sauce over medium heat in a large skillet.
4. Add the cooked pasta to the skillet with the pesto sauce.
Toss everything together until the pasta is coated with the sauce and heated.
5. Remove from heat and serve the pesto pasta immediately.

Nutritional Information (per serving): 460 calories, 13g protein, 43g carbohydrates, 27g fat, 6g fiber, 5mg cholesterol, 220mg sodium, 310mg potassium.

EGGPLANT AND TOMATO PASTA

INGREDIENTS

- 6 ounces spaghetti
- 1 medium eggplant, diced
- 2 tablespoons olive oil
- 2 cloves garlic, minced
- 1 can (14 ounces) diced tomatoes, drained
- 1/2 teaspoon dried oregano
- Salt and black pepper to taste
- Grated Parmesan cheese for serving (optional)

2

10 mins

20 mins

DIRECTIONS

1. Cook the spaghetti according to package instructions until al dente. Drain and set aside.
2. Heat olive oil over medium heat in a large skillet. Add minced garlic and sliced eggplant.. Cook until the eggplant is tender, about 8-10 minutes.
3. Add the drained diced tomatoes to the skillet and dried oregano, salt, and black pepper. Stir well to combine.
4. Cook the tomato and eggplant mixture for another 57 minutes, allowing the flavors to meld together.
5. Add the cooked spaghetti to the skillet with the eggplant and tomato sauce. Toss everything together until the pasta is evenly coated with the sauce.
6. Serve the Eggplant and Tomato Pasta hot, garnished with grated Parmesan cheese if desired.

Nutritional Information (per serving): 380 calories, 9g protein, 60g carbohydrates, 12g fat, 7g fiber, 0mg cholesterol, 320mg sodium, 550mg potassium.

LEMON GARLIC SHRIMP PASTA

INGREDIENTS

2

15 mins

15 mins

- 6 ounces whole wheat spaghetti
- 8 ounces shrimp, peeled and deveined
- 2 tablespoons olive oil
- 3 cloves garlic, minced
- Zest of 1 lemon
- Juice of 1 lemon
- Salt and pepper to taste
- Fresh parsley for garnish

DIRECTIONS

1. Cook the whole wheat spaghetti according to package instructions until al dente. Drain and set aside.
2. In a large skillet, heat olive oil over medium heat. Add minced garlic and sauté until fragrant.
3. Add the shrimp to the skillet until pink and cooked through, about 2-3 minutes per side.
4. Add lemon zest and juice to the skillet with the shrimp, seasoning with salt and pepper to taste.
5. Add the cooked spaghetti to the skillet with the shrimp and toss everything together until well combined.
6. Serve the lemon-garlic shrimp pasta hot, garnished with fresh parsley.

Nutritional Information (per serving): 450 calories, 30g protein, 40g carbohydrates, 18g fat, 4g fiber, 180mg cholesterol, 300mg sodium, 350mg potassium.

PASTA PUTTANESCA

INGREDIENTS

- 6 ounces spaghetti
- 2 tablespoons olive oil; 3 cloves garlic, minced
- 2 anchovy fillets, chopped (optional)
- 1/4 teaspoon red pepper flakes
- 1 can (15 ounces) diced tomatoes, drained
- 1/4 cup sliced Kalamata olives
- 2 tablespoons capers, drained
- 1/4 cup chopped fresh parsley
- Salt and black pepper to taste
- Grated Parmesan cheese for serving (optional)

2

10 mins

20 mins

DIRECTIONS

1. Cook the spaghetti according to package instructions until al dente. Drain and set aside.
2. Heat olive oil over medium heat in a large skillet. Add minced garlic, chopped anchovy fillets (if using), and red pepper flakes. Cook until the garlic is fragrant and the anchovies start to dissolve.
3. Add the diced tomatoes, sliced olives, and drained capers to the skillet. Cook for about 10 minutes, stirring occasionally, until the sauce thickens slightly.
4. Add the cooked spaghetti to the skillet with the sauce. Toss everything together until the pasta is well coated with the sauce.
5. Stir in chopped fresh parsley and season with salt and black pepper to taste.
6. If desired, Serve the pasta puttanesca hot, garnished with grated Parmesan cheese.

Nutritional Information (per serving): 450 calories, 12g protein, 60g carbohydrates, 18g fat, 5g fiber, 5mg cholesterol, 750mg sodium, 300mg potassium.

MEDITERRANEAN PASTA WITH ARTICHOKES AND SUNDRIED TOMATOES

INGREDIENTS

2

10 mins

15 mins

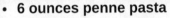

- 6 ounces penne pasta
- 1 tablespoon olive oil; 2 cloves garlic, minced
- 1/4 cup sundried tomatoes, chopped
- 1 can (14 ounces) artichoke hearts, drained and chopped
- 1/4 cup chopped fresh basil
- Salt and black pepper to taste
- Grated Parmesan cheese for serving (optional)

DIRECTIONS

1. Cook the penne pasta according to package instructions until al dente. Drain and set aside.
2. Heat olive oil over medium heat in a large skillet. Add minced garlic and chopped sundried tomatoes. Cook for 1-2 minutes until fragrant.
3. Add the chopped artichoke hearts to the skillet and cook for another 3-4 minutes until heated.
4. Add the cooked penne pasta to the skillet with the artichokes and sundried tomatoes. Toss everything together until well combined.
5. Stir in chopped fresh basil and season with salt and black pepper to taste.
6. Serve the Mediterranean pasta hot, garnished with grated Parmesan cheese if desired.

Nutritional Information (per serving): 420 calories, 12g protein, 55g carbohydrates, 18g fat, 5g fiber, 5mg cholesterol, 500mg sodium, 300mg potassium.

• SAUCES •

CLASSIC TOMATO SAUCE

INGREDIENTS

- 1 can (14 ounces) diced tomatoes
- 2 tablespoons olive oil
- 2 cloves garlic, minced
- 1/2 teaspoon dried oregano
- Salt and pepper to taste
- Fresh basil leaves, chopped (optional)

2

10 mins

20 mins

DIRECTIONS   IT IS IDEAL FOR PASTA DISHES LIKE SPAGHETTI OR AS A BASE FOR PIZZA.

1. Heat olive oil in a saucepan over medium heat. Add minced garlic and sauté until fragrant, about 1 minute.

2. Add the diced tomatoes and their juices. Stir in dried oregano, salt, and pepper. Bring the sauce to a simmer.

3. Reduce heat to low and let the sauce cook uncovered for about 15-20 minutes, stirring occasionally, until it thickens to your desired consistency.

4. If using fresh basil, stir it into the sauce before serving.

Nutritional Information (per serving): 120 calories, 2g protein, 9g carbohydrates, 9g fat, 2g fiber, 0mg cholesterol, 300mg sodium, 400mg potassium.

LEMON HERB VINAIGRETTE

INGREDIENTS

2

5 mins

0 mins

- 2 tablespoons fresh lemon juice
- 1/4 cup extra virgin olive oil
- 1 teaspoon Dijon mustard
- 1 clove garlic, minced
- 1/2 teaspoon dried oregano
- Salt and pepper to taste

DIRECTIONS   PERFECT FOR DRIZZLING OVER SALADS OR MARINATING GRILLED VEGETABLES.

1. In a small bowl, whisk together lemon juice, olive oil, Dijon mustard, minced garlic, dried oregano, salt, and pepper until well combined.

2. Taste and adjust seasoning according to your preference, adding more salt, pepper, or lemon juice if desired.

3. Use immediately as a salad dressing or a marinade for grilled vegetables or protein.

Nutritional Information (per serving): 180 calories, 0g protein, 1g carbohydrates, 20g fat, 0g fiber, 0mg cholesterol, 100mg sodium, 20mg potassium.

TZATZIKI SAUCE

INGREDIENTS

- 1/2 English cucumber, grated, and excess moisture squeezed out
- 1 cup plain Greek yogurt
- 1 clove garlic, minced
- 1 tablespoon fresh dill, chopped
- 1 tablespoon fresh lemon juice
- Salt and pepper to taste

2

10 mins

0 mins

DIRECTIONS   GOES WELL WITH GYROS, GRILLED MEATS, OR AS A DIP FOR PITA BREAD AND VEGGIES.

1. Grate the cucumber using a box grater and squeeze out excess moisture using a clean kitchen towel or paper towel.

2. In a bowl, combine the grated cucumber, Greek yogurt, minced garlic, chopped dill, lemon juice, salt, and pepper. Mix well until thoroughly combined.

3. Taste and adjust seasoning as needed, adding more salt, pepper, or lemon juice if desired.

4. Serve immediately as a dip for vegetables spread for sandwiches or sauce for grilled meats.

Nutritional Information (per serving): 70 calories, 7g protein, 8g carbohydrates, 1g fat, 1g fiber, 5mg cholesterol, 40mg sodium, 250mg potassium.

CHIMICHURRI SAUCE

INGREDIENTS

2

10 mins

0 mins

- 1 cup fresh parsley, chopped
- 1/4 cup fresh cilantro, chopped
- 2 cloves garlic, minced
- 2 tablespoons red wine vinegar
- 1/4 cup extra virgin olive oil
- 1/4 teaspoon red pepper flakes (optional)
- Salt and pepper to taste

DIRECTIONS   GREAT FOR TOPPING GRILLED STEAKS, CHICKEN, OR FISH.

1. In a bowl, combine the chopped parsley, chopped cilantro, minced garlic, red wine vinegar, and optional red pepper flakes.

2. Slowly drizzle in the extra virgin olive oil while stirring to combine.

3. Season with salt and pepper to taste, adjusting the seasoning as needed.

4. Let the chimichurri sauce sit for at least 10 minutes to allow the flavors to meld together before serving.

Nutritional Information (per serving): 260 calories, 2g protein, 4g carbohydrates, 27g fat, 1g fiber, 0mg cholesterol, 5mg sodium, 350mg potassium.

ROASTED RED PEPPER SAUCE

INGREDIENTS

- 2 large red bell peppers
- 2 tablespoons olive oil
- 1 small onion, chopped
- 2 cloves garlic, minced
- 1/2 teaspoon dried basil
- Salt and pepper to taste

2

10 mins

25 mins

DIRECTIONS
DELICIOUS SERVED OVER PASTA, GRILLED CHICKEN, OR AS A DIP FOR CRUSTY BREAD.

1. Preheat the oven to 400°F (200°C). Line a baking sheet with parchment paper.
2. Cut the red bell peppers in half and remove the seeds and stems. Place them cut-side down on the prepared baking sheet. Roast the peppers in the oven for about 20-25 minutes or until the skins are charred and blistered.
3. Remove the peppers from the oven and let them cool slightly. Peel off the charred skin and discard.
4. Heat olive oil over medium heat in a saucepan. Add chopped onion and minced garlic. Sauté until the onion is translucent, about 5 minutes.
5. Chop the roasted red peppers and add them to the saucepan along with dried basil, salt, and pepper. Cook for another 5 minutes, stirring occasionally.
6. Transfer the mixture to a blender or food processor and blend until smooth.
7. Serve the roasted red pepper sauce over pasta, grilled vegetables, or as a dip.

Nutritional Information (per serving): 160 calories, 2g protein, 10g carbohydrates, 13g fat, 3g fiber, 0mg cholesterol, 250mg sodium, 350mg potassium.

OLIVE TAPENADE SAUCE

INGREDIENTS

2

10 mins

5 mins

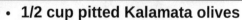

- 1/2 cup pitted Kalamata olives
- 1/4 cup pitted green olives
- 1 tablespoon capers, drained
- 1 clove garlic, minced
- 2 tablespoons extra virgin olive oil
- 1 teaspoon fresh lemon juice
- Freshly ground black pepper, to taste

DIRECTIONS
PERFECT SPREAD FOR SANDWICHES, TOPPING FOR BRUSCHETTA, OR AS A DIP FOR CRACKERS.

1. Combine the pitted Kalamata olives, pitted green olives, drained capers, and minced garlic in a food processor.
2. Pulse the mixture until it becomes a coarse paste.
3. While pulsing, slowly drizzle in the extra virgin olive oil and fresh lemon juice until the tapenade reaches your desired consistency.
4. Season with freshly ground black pepper to taste.
5. Transfer the olive tapenade to a bowl and serve as a spread for bread, topping for grilled meats or fish, or as a dip for vegetables.

Nutritional Information (per serving): 150 calories, 1g protein, 4g carbohydrates, 15g fat, 2g fiber, 0mg cholesterol, 600mg sodium, 100mg potassium.

BASIL PESTO SAUCE

INGREDIENTS

- 2 cups fresh basil leaves, packed
- 1/2 cup grated Parmesan cheese
- 1/3 cup extra virgin olive oil
- 1/4 cup pine nuts or walnuts, toasted
- 2 cloves garlic, minced
- Salt and pepper to taste

2

10 mins

0 mins

DIRECTIONS   CLASSIC SAUCE FOR PASTA DISHES, PIZZA, OR AS A SPREAD FOR SANDWICHES.

1. Combine the fresh basil leaves, grated Parmesan cheese, toasted pine nuts or walnuts, minced garlic, salt, and pepper in a food processor.

2. Pulse the ingredients until roughly chopped.

3. While the food processor is running, slowly drizzle in the extra virgin olive oil until the pesto reaches a smooth and creamy consistency.

4. Taste and adjust seasoning as needed, adding more salt, pepper, or Parmesan cheese if desired.

5. Transfer the basil pesto sauce to a jar or bowl and refrigerate until ready.

Nutritional Information (per serving): 400 calories, 10g protein, 5g carbohydrates, 40g fat, 2g fiber, 10mg cholesterol, 200mg sodium, 300mg potassium.

GARLIC YOGURT SAUCE

INGREDIENTS

2

5 mins

0 mins

- 1 cup plain Greek yogurt
- 2 cloves garlic, minced
- 1 tablespoon fresh lemon juice
- 1 tablespoon extra virgin olive oil
- Salt and pepper to taste
- Fresh parsley, chopped (optional garnish)

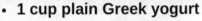

DIRECTIONS   IT IS EXCELLENT AS A VEGETABLE DIP, SAUCE FOR GRILLED MEATS, OR SALAD DRESSING.

1. In a bowl, combine the plain Greek yogurt, minced garlic, fresh lemon juice, and extra virgin olive oil.

2. Mix well until the ingredients are thoroughly combined.

3. Season the sauce with salt and pepper to taste, adjusting the seasoning as needed.

4. If desired, garnish with chopped fresh parsley before serving.

5. Serve the garlic yogurt sauce as a vegetable dip, sauce for grilled meats, or salad dressing.

Nutritional Information (per serving): 180 calories, 12g protein, 8g carbohydrates, 12g fat, 0g fiber, 10mg cholesterol, 80mg sodium, 250mg potassium.

SUNDRIED TOMATO PESTO SAUCE

INGREDIENTS

- 1/2 cup sundried tomatoes (packed in oil), drained
- 1/4 cup grated Parmesan cheese
- 1/4 cup pine nuts or walnuts, toasted
- 2 cloves garlic, minced
- 1/4 cup extra virgin olive oil
- Salt and pepper to taste

2

10 mins

0 mins

DIRECTIONS
IT IS IDEAL FOR TOSSING WITH PASTA, TOPPING FOR GRILLED CHICKEN, OR SPREAD ON CROSTINI.

1. Combine sundried tomatoes, grated Parmesan cheese, toasted pine nuts or walnuts, and minced garlic in a food processor.

2. Pulse the ingredients until well combined and a thick paste forms.

3. While the food processor is running, slowly drizzle in the extra virgin olive oil until the pesto reaches your desired consistency.

4. Season with salt and pepper to taste, adjusting the seasoning as needed.

5. Transfer the sundried tomato pesto sauce to a jar or bowl and refrigerate until ready to use.

Nutritional Information (per serving): 350 calories, 8g protein, 10g carbohydrates, 32g fat, 3g fiber, 10mg cholesterol, 300mg sodium, 450mg potassium.

CAPER AND LEMON SAUCE

INGREDIENTS

2

5 mins

5 mins

- 2 tablespoons capers, drained and chopped
- 2 tablespoons fresh lemon juice
- 2 tablespoons extra virgin olive oil
- 1 clove garlic, minced
- Salt and pepper to taste
- Fresh parsley, chopped (optional garnish)

DIRECTIONS
GREAT WITH SEAFOOD DISHES LIKE GRILLED FISH OR SHRIMP SCAMPI.

1. Heat the extra virgin olive oil over medium heat in a small saucepan.

2. Add minced garlic and sauté until fragrant, about 1 minute.

3. Stir in the chopped capers and fresh lemon juice. Cook for 2-3 minutes, allowing the flavors to meld together.

4. Season the sauce with salt and pepper to taste, adjusting the seasoning as needed.

5. If desired, garnish with chopped fresh parsley before serving.

Nutritional Information (per serving): 120 calories, 1g protein, 3g carbohydrates, 12g fat, 1g fiber, 0mg cholesterol, 500mg sodium, 100mg potassium.

MUSHROOM MARSALA SAUCE

INGREDIENTS

- 1 tablespoon olive oil
- 1 cup sliced mushrooms
- 2 cloves garlic, minced
- 1/4 cup Marsala wine
- 1/2 cup vegetable broth
- 1/4 cup heavy cream
- Salt and pepper to taste
- Fresh parsley, chopped (optional garnish)

2

10 mins

15 mins

DIRECTIONS
DELICIOUSLY SERVED OVER PASTA, CHICKEN, OR AS A SAUCE FOR BEEF DISHES.

1. Heat olive oil over medium heat in a skillet. Add sliced mushrooms and minced garlic. Sauté until the mushrooms are golden brown and tender, about 5-7 minutes.

2. Pour in Marsala wine and cook for 2-3 minutes to allow the alcohol to evaporate and the flavors to blend.

3. Add vegetable broth to the skillet and simmer for another 5 minutes, allowing the sauce to reduce slightly.

4. Stir in heavy cream and season with salt and pepper to taste. Simmer for an additional 2-3 minutes until the sauce thickens slightly.

5. Garnish with chopped fresh parsley before serving.

Nutritional Information (per serving): 250 calories, 4g protein, 8g carbohydrates, 20g fat, 1g fiber, 50mg cholesterol, 300mg sodium, 400mg potassium.

WHITE BEAN AND GARLIC SAUCE

INGREDIENTS

2

5 mins

5 mins

- 1 can (15 ounces) white beans, drained and rinsed
- 2 tablespoons olive oil
- 2 cloves garlic, minced
- 1/2 cup vegetable broth
- 1 tablespoon fresh lemon juice
- Salt and pepper to taste
- Fresh parsley, chopped (optional garnish)

DIRECTIONS

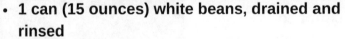

DELICIOUSLY SERVED OVER PASTA, CHICKEN, OR AS A SAUCE FOR BEEF DISHES.

1. Heat olive oil over medium heat in a saucepan. Add minced garlic and sauté until fragrant, about 1 minute.

2. Add the drained and rinsed white beans to the saucepan. Stir and cook for 2-3 minutes to heat through.

3. Add vegetable broth and fresh lemon juice. Bring the mixture to a simmer and let it cook for 5-7 minutes, allowing the flavors to meld.

4. Using a potato masher or fork, mash some beans to thicken the sauce while leaving some whole beans for texture. Season with salt and pepper to taste. Garnish with chopped fresh parsley before serving.

Nutritional Information (per serving): 280 calories, 10g protein, 35g carbohydrates, 12g fat, 8g fiber, 0mg cholesterol, 450mg sodium, 650mg potassium.

• SNACKS •

ALMONDS AND DRIED FRUIT MIX

INGREDIENTS

- 1/2 cup raw almonds
- 1/4 cup dried apricots, chopped
- 1/4 cup dried cranberries
- 1/4 cup golden raisins
- 1/4 teaspoon ground cinnamon (optional)

2

5 mins

0 mins

DIRECTIONS

1. In a mixing bowl, combine the raw almonds, dried apricots, dried cranberries, golden raisins, and ground cinnamon (if using).
2. Toss the ingredients together until well combined.
3. Divide the mixture into two servings or transfer to an airtight container for storage.
4. Enjoy as a nutritious snack or add to yogurt or salads for extra flavor and texture.

Nutritional Information (per serving): 280 calories, 7g protein, 37g carbohydrates, 14g fat, 6g fiber, 0mg cholesterol, 0mg sodium, 380mg potassium.

WHOLE GRAIN CRACKERS WITH OLIVE TAPENADE

INGREDIENTS

2

10 mins

0 mins

- 8 whole grain crackers
- 1/2 cup pitted black olives, chopped
- 1 tablespoon capers, drained and chopped
- 1 tablespoon extra virgin olive oil
- 1 small garlic clove, minced
- 1 tablespoon chopped fresh parsley
- Salt and pepper to taste

DIRECTIONS

1. In a bowl, combine the chopped black olives, capers, minced garlic, chopped parsley, extra virgin olive oil, salt, and pepper. Mix well to make the olive tapenade.
2. Spread the olive tapenade evenly onto each wholegrain cracker.
3. Arrange the crackers on a serving plate.
4. Serve the whole grain crackers with olive tapenade as a delicious and healthy snack or appetizer.

Nutritional Information (per serving): 170 calories, 3g protein, 16g carbohydrates, 11g fat, 4g fiber, 0mg cholesterol, 420mg sodium, 160mg potassium.

PITA BREAD WITH TZATZIKI

INGREDIENTS

- 2 whole wheat pita bread rounds
- 1/2 cup plain Greek yogurt
- 1/2 cucumber, peeled, seeded, and grated
- 1 small garlic clove, minced
- 1 tablespoon fresh lemon juice
- 1 tablespoon chopped fresh dill (or one teaspoon dried dill)
- Salt and pepper to taste

2
10 mins
5 mins

DIRECTIONS

1. In a bowl, combine the Greek yogurt, grated cucumber, minced garlic, fresh lemon juice, chopped dill, salt, and pepper. Mix well to make the tzatziki sauce.
2. Warm the pita bread rounds in a toaster or oven until slightly crispy.
3. Cut each pita bread round in half to form pockets.
4. Stuff each pita pocket with a generous amount of tzatziki sauce.
5. Serve the pita bread with tzatziki as a tasty and satisfying Mediterranean snack or light meal.

Nutritional Information (per serving): 190 calories, 9g protein, 34g carbohydrates, 2g fat, 4g fiber, 0mg cholesterol, 220mg sodium, 260mg potassium.

BRUSCHETTA

INGREDIENTS

2
10 mins
5 mins

- 4 slices of whole-grain bread
- 2 ripe tomatoes, diced
- 1 clove garlic, minced
- 2 tablespoons extra virgin olive oil
- 1 tablespoon balsamic vinegar
- Salt and pepper to taste
- Fresh basil leaves, chopped (optional)

DIRECTIONS

1. Preheat a grill pan or skillet over medium heat.
2. In a bowl, combine the diced tomatoes, minced garlic, extra virgin olive oil, balsamic vinegar, salt, and pepper. Mix well to make the bruschetta topping.
3. Grill the slices of whole grain bread on the preheated grill pan or skillet until lightly toasted on both sides, about 2-3 minutes per side.
4. Remove the toasted bread from the heat and top each slice with the bruschetta topping.
5. Garnish with chopped fresh basil leaves, if desired, and serve immediately.

Nutritional Information (per serving): 270 calories, 6g protein, 34g carbohydrates, 13g fat, 5g fiber, 0mg cholesterol, 400mg sodium, 300mg potassium.

ROASTED CHICKPEAS

INGREDIENTS

- 1 can (15 ounces) chickpeas, drained and rinsed
- 1 tablespoon olive oil
- 1 teaspoon paprika
- 1/2 teaspoon cumin
- 1/2 teaspoon garlic powder
- Salt and pepper to taste

2

5 mins

20 mins

DIRECTIONS

1. Preheat your oven to 400°F (200°C).

2. Pat dry the chickpeas using a paper towel to remove excess moisture.

3. Toss the chickpeas with olive oil, paprika, cumin, garlic powder, salt, and pepper until evenly coated.

4. Spread the seasoned chickpeas in a single layer on a baking sheet lined with parchment paper.

5. Roast in the preheated oven for about 20 minutes or until golden brown and crispy, shaking the pan halfway through to ensure even cooking.

Nutritional Information (per serving): 240 calories, 9g protein, 30g carbohydrates, 10g fat, 6g fiber, 0mg cholesterol, 370mg sodium, 340mg potassium.

• DESSERTS •

YOGURT FRUIT SMOOTHIE

INGREDIENTS

- 1 cup plain Greek yogurt
- 1/2 cup mixed fresh or frozen fruits (such as berries, banana, mango)
- 1/2 cup unsweetened almond milk (or any milk
- of your choice)
- 1 tablespoon honey or maple syrup (optional)
- Ice cubes (optional)

2

5 mins

0 mins

DIRECTIONS

1. In a blender, combine the plain Greek yogurt, mixed fruits, almond milk, and honey or maple syrup (if using).
2. Add ice cubes to the blender for a colder and thicker smoothie.
3. Blend until smooth and creamy.
4. Pour the smoothie into glasses and serve immediately

Nutritional Information (per serving): 150 calories, 10g protein, 20g carbohydrates, 4g fat, 3g fiber, 5mg cholesterol, 70mg sodium, 250mg potassium.

BAKED OATMEAL CUPS

INGREDIENTS

2

10 mins

20 mins

- 1 cup oldfashioned oats
- 1 ripe banana, mashed
- 1/2 cup milk (dairy or nondairy)
- 1 tablespoon honey or maple syrup
- 1/2 teaspoon vanilla extract
- 1/2 teaspoon ground cinnamon;
- 1/4 teaspoon salt
- Optional toppings: fresh berries, chopped nuts, shredded coconut

DIRECTIONS

1. Preheat your oven to 350°F (175°C) and grease a muffin tin with cooking spray or line it with muffin liners.
2. Combine the oldfashioned oats, mashed banana, milk, honey or maple syrup, vanilla extract, ground cinnamon, and salt in a bowl. Mix until well combined.
3. Divide the oat mixture evenly among the muffin cups, filling each about 2/3 full.
4. Press lightly on each cup's oat mixture to flatten the tops.
5. Bake the oatmeal cups in the oven for about 20 minutes or until set and lightly golden on top.
6. Remove the oatmeal cups from the oven and let them cool in the muffin tin for a few minutes before transferring them to a wire rack to cool completely.
7. Once cooled, Top the oatmeal cups with fresh berries, chopped nuts, or shredded coconut.

Nutritional Information (per serving): 200 calories, 6g protein, 35g carbohydrates, 4g fat, 5g fiber, 5mg cholesterol, 150mg sodium, 250mg potassium.

BAKED PEARS WITH CINNAMON

INGREDIENTS

- 2 ripe pears, halved and cored
- 1 tablespoon honey
- 1/2 teaspoon ground cinnamon
- 1/4 teaspoon ground nutmeg
- 1 tablespoon chopped nuts (such as walnuts or almonds)

2

10 mins

25 mins

DIRECTIONS

1. Preheat the oven to 375°F (190°C).
2. Place the pear halves cut side up in a baking dish.
3. Drizzle honey over the pears and sprinkle with ground cinnamon and nutmeg.
4. Cover the baking dish with foil and bake for 20 minutes.
5. Remove the foil, sprinkle chopped nuts over the pears, and bake uncovered for 5 minutes or until the pears are tender.

Nutritional Information (per serving): 150 calories, 1g protein, 38g carbohydrates, 1g fat, 6g fiber, 0mg cholesterol, 0mg sodium, 250mg potassium.

FIG AND ALMOND ENERGY BALLS

INGREDIENTS

2

10 mins

0 mins

- 1/2 cup dried figs
- 1/2 cup almonds
- 1 tablespoon honey
- 1/2 teaspoon vanilla extract
- Pinch of salt

DIRECTIONS

1. In a food processor, combine the dried figs, almonds, honey, vanilla extract, and a pinch of salt.
2. Pulse until the mixture comes together and forms a sticky dough.
3. Scoop out tablespoon-sized portions of the mixture and roll them into balls using your hands.
4. Place the energy balls on a plate or baking sheet lined with parchment paper.
5. Refrigerate the energy balls for at least 30 minutes before serving.

Nutritional Information (per serving): 90 calories, 2g protein, 11g carbohydrates, 5g fat, 2g fiber, 0mg cholesterol, 0mg sodium, 150mg potassium.

ORANGE AND ALMOND CAKE

INGREDIENTS

- 1 large orange
- 1/2 cup almond meal
- 1/4 cup honey or maple syrup
- 2 eggs
- 1 teaspoon baking powder

2

15 mins

30 mins

DIRECTIONS

1. Preheat the oven to 350°F (175°C) and grease a small cake pan.
2. Cut the orange into quarters, remove any seeds, and blend it in a food processor until smooth.
3. In a mixing bowl, combine the blended orange, almond meal, honey or maple syrup, eggs, and baking powder. Mix until well combined.
4. Pour the batter into the greased cake pan and smooth the top.
5. Bake in the preheated oven for about 25-30 minutes or until a toothpick inserted into the center comes out clean.

Nutritional Information (per serving): 280 calories, 9g protein, 23g carbohydrates, 18g fat, 4g fiber, 186mg cholesterol, 134mg sodium, 330mg potassium.

POACHED APRICOTS IN SYRUP

INGREDIENTS

2

5 mins

10 mins

- 4 fresh apricots, halved and pitted
- 1/2 cup water
- 1/4 cup honey or maple syrup
- 1/2 teaspoon vanilla extract
- 1 cinnamon stick (optional)

DIRECTIONS

1. In a saucepan, combine water, honey or maple syrup, vanilla extract, and cinnamon stick (if using). Bring to a simmer over medium heat.
2. Add the apricot halves to the simmering syrup and cut the side down.
3. Cook the apricots for about 5 minutes, then gently flip them over and continue to cook for another 5 minutes or until they are tender but not mushy.
4. Remove the poached apricots from the syrup and serve warm or chilled, drizzled with the syrup.

Nutritional Information (per serving): 120 calories, 1g protein, 31g carbohydrates, 0g fat, 2g fiber, 0mg cholesterol, 0mg sodium, 300mg potassium.

LEMON SORBET

INGREDIENTS

- 1 cup water
- 1/2 cup granulated sugar
- Zest of 1 lemon
- 1/2 cup fresh lemon juice (about 3-4 lemons)

2

10 mins

0 mins

DIRECTIONS

1. Combine water, granulated sugar, and lemon zest in a small saucepan. Heat over medium heat, stirring occasionally, until the sugar dissolves completely and the mixture comes to a simmer.

2. Remove the saucepan from the heat and let the syrup cool to room temperature.

3. Stir in fresh lemon juice into the cooled syrup.

4. Place the lemon syrup mixture into a shallow dish or container in the freezer.

5. Every 30 minutes, use a fork to scrape and stir the mixture to break up any ice crystals until it reaches a sorbet consistency, about 2-3 hours.

Nutritional Information (per serving): 130 calories, 0g protein, 33g carbohydrates, 0g fat, 0g fiber, 0mg cholesterol, 0mg sodium, 30mg potassium.

RICOTTA AND HONEY TOAST

INGREDIENTS

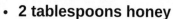
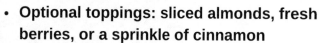

2

5 mins

5 mins

- 4 slices of whole-grain bread
- 1/2 cup ricotta cheese
- 2 tablespoons honey
- Optional toppings: sliced almonds, fresh berries, or a sprinkle of cinnamon

DIRECTIONS

1. Toast the slices of whole grain bread until golden brown and crispy.

2. Spread ricotta cheese evenly on each toasted slice.

3. Drizzle honey over the ricotta cheese.

4. Add optional toppings such as sliced almonds, fresh berries, or a sprinkle of cinnamon.

5. Serve the ricotta and honey toast immediately as a delicious and satisfying breakfast or snack.

Nutritional Information (per serving): 250 calories, 11g protein, 35g carbohydrates, 7g fat, 5g fiber, 15mg cholesterol, 250mg sodium, 180mg potassium.

FRESH FRUIT SALAD

INGREDIENTS

- 1 cup fresh mixed fruits (such as strawberries, blueberries, grapes, and kiwi), chopped
- 1 tablespoon honey or maple syrup (optional)
- Fresh mint leaves for garnish (optional)

2

10 mins

0 mins

DIRECTIONS

1. Wash and chop the mixed fruits into bite-sized pieces.
2. In a bowl, combine the chopped fruits.
3. Drizzle honey or maple syrup over the fruit for added sweetness if desired.
4. Gently toss the fruit salad until well combined.
5. If using fresh mint leaves, garnish and serve immediately or refrigerate until ready to serve.

Nutritional Information (per serving): 120 calories, 1g protein, 30g carbohydrates, 0g fat, 3g fiber, 0mg cholesterol, 0mg sodium, 250mg potassium.

GREEK YOGURT PARFAIT

INGREDIENTS

2

10 mins

10 mins

- 1 cup plain Greek yogurt
- 1/2 cup granola
- 1/2 cup mixed fresh berries (such as strawberries, blueberries, raspberries)
- 2 tablespoons honey or maple syrup (optional)
- Fresh mint leaves for garnish (optional)

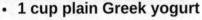

DIRECTIONS

1. Layer the plain Greek yogurt, granola, and mixed fresh berries in two serving glasses or bowls.
2. Repeat the layers until all ingredients are used, ending with a layer of berries on top.
3. Drizzle honey or maple syrup over the parfait for added sweetness, if desired.
4. Garnish with fresh mint leaves if using.
5. Serve the Greek yogurt parfait immediately as a delicious and nutritious breakfast or snack.

Nutritional Information (per serving): 280 calories, 15g protein, 40g carbohydrates, 8g fat, 4g fiber, 10mg cholesterol, 60mg sodium, 250mg potassium.

FROZEN YOGURT BARK

INGREDIENTS

- 1 cup plain Greek yogurt
- 2 tablespoons honey or maple syrup
- 1/2 teaspoon vanilla extract
- 1/4 cup mixed fresh berries (such as strawberries, blueberries, raspberries)
- 2 tablespoons chopped nuts (such as almonds and walnuts)

2

10 mins

0 mins

DIRECTIONS

1. Mix the plain Greek yogurt, honey or maple syrup, and vanilla extract until well combined.
2. Line a baking sheet with parchment paper.
3. Spread the yogurt mixture evenly on the parchment paper to form a thin layer.
4. Sprinkle the mixed fresh berries and chopped nuts over the yogurt layer.
5. Place the baking sheet in the freezer for at least 2 hours or until the yogurt bark is completely frozen.
6. Once frozen, break the yogurt bark into pieces and serve immediately as a refreshing and healthy snack.

Nutritional Information (per serving): 190 calories, 9g protein, 25g carbohydrates, 7g fat, 2g fiber, 10mg cholesterol, 50mg sodium, 250mg potassium.

CHIA SEED PUDDING

INGREDIENTS

2

5 mins

0 mins

- 1/4 cup chia seeds
- 1 cup unsweetened almond milk (or any milk of your choice)
- 1 tablespoon honey or maple syrup (optional)
- 1/2 teaspoon vanilla extract
- Fresh fruits or nuts for topping (optional)

DIRECTIONS

1. In a bowl, combine the chia seeds, almond milk, honey or maple syrup (if using), and vanilla extract.
2. Mix well to ensure the chia seeds are evenly distributed.
3. Cover the bowl and refrigerate for at least 2 hours or overnight, allowing the chia seeds to absorb the liquid and form a pudding-like consistency.
4. Stir the chia seed pudding before serving and top with fresh fruits or nuts, if desired.

Nutritional Information (per serving): 160 calories, 4g protein, 15g carbohydrates, 9g fat, 9g fiber, 0mg cholesterol, 80mg sodium, 150mg potassium.

DARK CHOCOLATE DIPPED STRAWBERRIES

INGREDIENTS

- 8 large strawberries, washed and dried
- 2 ounces dark chocolate, chopped
- 1 teaspoon coconut oil
- Optional toppings: chopped nuts, shredded coconut, or sea salt flakes

2

10 mins

5 mins

DIRECTIONS

1. Line a baking sheet with parchment paper.

2. Combine dark chocolate and coconut oil in a microwavesafe bowl. Microwave in 30-second intervals, stirring in between, until the chocolate is melted and smooth.

3. Hold each strawberry by the stem and dip it into the melted chocolate, coating about three-quarters.

4. Place the dipped strawberries on the prepared baking sheet.

5. If using optional toppings, sprinkle them over the chocolate-covered parts of the strawberries. Refrigerate the strawberries for about 15 minutes or until the chocolate is set.

Nutritional Information (per serving): 120 calories, 2g protein, 14g carbohydrates, 7g fat, 3g fiber, 0mg cholesterol, 0mg sodium, 200mg potassium.

ALMOND DATE BALLS

INGREDIENTS

2

10 mins

0 mins

- 1/2 cup almonds
- 1/2 cup pitted dates
- 1 tablespoon unsweetened shredded coconut
- 1/2 teaspoon vanilla extract
- Pinch of salt

DIRECTIONS

1. In a food processor, combine the almonds, pitted dates, shredded coconut, vanilla extract, and a pinch of salt.

2. Pulse the mixture until it forms a sticky doughlike consistency.

3. Scoop out tablespoon-sized portions of the mixture and roll them into balls using your hands.

4. Place the almond date balls on a plate or baking sheet lined with parchment paper.

5. Refrigerate the balls for at least 30 minutes before serving.

Nutritional Information (per serving): 150 calories, 4g protein, 20g carbohydrates, 8g fat, 4g fiber, 0mg cholesterol, 0mg sodium, 250mg potassium.

30-DAY MEAL PLAN

DAYS	BREAKFAST	LUNCH	DINNER	CALORIC CONTENT
1	AVOCADO TOAST	GREEK SALAD	MEDITERRANEAN CHICKEN SKILLET	1600
2	MEDITERRANEAN VEGGIE OMELETTE	HUMMUS AND BABA GANOUSH WITH GRILLED VEGETABLES	MEDITERRANEAN BEEF KEBABS WITH TZATZIKI	1700
3	QUINOA BREAKFAST BOWL	MEDITERRANEAN LENTIL SALAD	GREEK MOUSSAKA	1800
4	CHIA SEED PUDDING	MEDITERRANEAN CHICKPEA SALAD	BAKED WHOLE FISH WITH ROASTED VEGETABLES	1600
5	RICOTTA AND FIG TOAST	CAPRESE SALAD	MEDITERRANEAN LAMB STEW	1750
6	OATMEAL WITH MEDITERRANEAN TOPPINGS	MEDITERRANEAN CUCUMBER SALAD	MEDITERRANEAN SHRIMP PASTA	1700
7	ALMOND BUTTER AND BANANA TOAST	MEDITERRANEAN BEET SALAD	EGGPLANT AND TOMATO PASTA	1750
8	MEDITERRANEAN-STYLE PANCAKES	MEDITERRANEAN GRAIN BOWLS WITH LENTILS AND CHICKPEAS	MEDITERRANEAN CHICKEN PIZZA	1800
9	SMOKED SALMON PLATE	CHICKPEA STEW	GRILLED SALMON WITH LEMON AND HERBS	1700
10	FETA AND OLIVE FRITTATA, GREEK YOGURT WITH HONEY AND NUTS	MEDITERRANEAN COUSCOUS SALAD	MEDITERRANEAN SEAFOOD PIZZA	1750
11	MEDITERRANEAN SHAKSHUKA	ROASTED VEGETABLES	CHICKEN SKILLET WITH MUSHROOMS AND SLIVERED PARMESAN	1800
12	HONEY-SPICED GRANOLA WITH YOGURT	HUMMUS AND BABA GANOUSH WITH GRILLED VEGETABLES	SEAFOOD PAELLA	1700
13	PISTACHIO AND HONEY TOAST	MEDITERRANEAN KALE SALAD	LINGUINE WITH CLAMS	1750
14	AVOCADO TOAST	QUINOA TABBOULEH SALAD	MEDITERRANEAN BEEF STEW	1800
15	GREEK SCRAMBLED EGGS (STRAPATSADA)	MEDITERRANEAN LENTIL SALAD	GREEK PIZZA	1700

30-DAY MEAL PLAN

DAYS	BREAKFAST	LUNCH	DINNER	CALORIC CONTENT
16	MEDITERRANEAN VEGGIE OMELETTE	MEDITERRANEAN CHICKPEA SALAD	GREEK MOUSSAKA	1750
17	CHIA SEED PUDDING	GREEK SALAD	BAKED WHOLE FISH WITH ROASTED VEGETABLES	1600
18	RICOTTA AND FIG TOAST	MEDITERRANEAN LENTIL SALAD	MEDITERRANEAN LAMB STEW	1750
19	AVOCADO TOAST	CAPRESE SALAD	EGGPLANT AND TOMATO PASTA	1750
20	OATMEAL WITH MEDITERRANEAN TOPPINGS	MEDITERRANEAN CUCUMBER SALAD	MEDITERRANEAN SHRIMP PASTA	1700
21	ALMOND BUTTER AND BANANA TOAST	MEDITERRANEAN BEET SALAD	MEDITERRANEAN CHICKEN PIZZA	1750
22	MEDITERRANEAN-STYLE PANCAKES	MEDITERRANEAN GRAIN BOWLS WITH LENTILS AND CHICKPEAS	SEAFOOD PAELLA	1800
23	SMOKED SALMON PLATE	CHICKPEA STEW	GRILLED SALMON WITH LEMON AND HERBS	1700
24	FETA AND OLIVE FRITTATA, GREEK YOGURT WITH HONEY AND NUTS	MEDITERRANEAN COUSCOUS SALAD	MEDITERRANEAN SEAFOOD PIZZA	1750
25	MEDITERRANEAN SHAKSHUKA	ROASTED VEGETABLES	CHICKEN SKILLET WITH MUSHROOMS AND SLIVERED PARMESAN	1800
26	HONEY-SPICED GRANOLA WITH YOGURT	HUMMUS AND BABA GANOUSH WITH GRILLED VEGETABLES	LINGUINE WITH CLAMS	1750
27	PISTACHIO AND HONEY TOAST	MEDITERRANEAN KALE SALAD	GREEK PIZZA	1700
28	GREEK SCRAMBLED EGGS (STRAPATSADA)	MEDITERRANEAN LENTIL SALAD	MEDITERRANEAN BEEF STEW	1800
29	MEDITERRANEAN VEGGIE OMELETTE	MEDITERRANEAN CHICKPEA SALAD	GREEK MOUSSAKA	1750
30	CHIA SEED PUDDING	GREEK SALAD	BAKED WHOLE FISH WITH ROASTED VEGETABLES	1600

Made in United States
Cleveland, OH
27 December 2024

12727077R00052